Folk Tales from the Land of the Mahabharata

DR. J.N. KAUSHIK
Ex. Director
Haryana Sahitya Akademy

SHIPRA

Price: Rs. 300.00, US$ 15.00

ISBN: 978-81-7541-450-1

First Published in India in 2012

Folk Tales from the Land of the Mahabharata

Published by :

SHIPRA PUBLICATIONS

H.O.: LG 18-19, Pankaj Central Market, Patparganj,
I.P. Ext., Delhi-110092, Tel: 91-11-2223 5152, 2223 6152
Br.Off.: 4617/18, Ansari Road, Darya Ganj,
New Delhi-110002, Tel: 6594 6453, 9810522367
E-mail: info@shiprapublications.com
www.shiprapublications.com

Contents

Introduction

Folktale is a general term for any of the numerous varieties of traditional narrative. Folktales are often stories of human beings and animals act like humans and that live in a world of wonder and magic. Most of these stories convey a message or moral to the reader or explain something in a creative way. They reflect human behaviour and thought process in their most natural form. Folktales are often passed down and retold from generation to generation by word of mouth.

Folktales are the forerunners of written literature, especially fiction and legends, all over the world. It is a mixture of tribal, pastoral and even modern traditions. It portrays human instinct in all its forms. Sometimes, human beings are very liberal, sympathetic, benevolent, adventurous, and forgiving and at other times they are just otherwise. Folktales are the real caricatures of human society in their different modes and moods. No folktale can be termed as good or bad on the basis of its theme. Different societies have their own traditions, which are framed by their natural environment and which then become the basis of their folktales.

The author of this volume had heard most of these stories 60 to 65 years back in his childhood and boyhood from members of his family and peer group in his own mother tongue, Haryanvi. The moods, gestures, intonations and places referred to in these tales are still fresh in his mind. In recounting them in this volume, he has tried to retain its original flavour by using local vocabulary, sentence constructions, quotes and even by rendering some rhythmic lores into verse, though with partial success because the words in translated language sometimes lack and falter.

The present collection of folktales forms an important part of world literature. It is from the land of the Mahabharata, the land of the Bhagwad Gita. The Mahabharata epic war was fought more than five thousand years ago The area of these folktales includes, Kuruvana or the jungles of that era and Kururkshetra – the seat of power of the Kauravas and the Pandavas—generally known as Indraprastha (Delhi) and Hastinapur (in Uttar Pradesh).

Some of these stories are related to lengendary characters like Lord Krishna, Daan Veer Karn, Lord Rama, Sita, Shravan Kumar, Dharmaraj Yudhishthira, Bhima, Draupadi, Vikram, Bhartrihari, Harnandi and Nalwa. All these stories are soaked with the tinge and colour of folklore. They present a variety of characters. Some of them are super-natural, other-worldly—gods , goddesses like Mahadeva-Parvati, Yama, Lakshmi etc. You will find in these stories devils, monsters and fairies as well. There are kings, queens, *wazirs* (ministers), *kotwals* (police inspectors) who act in their own way. On the other hand there are birds like swans, parrots, owls and animals like wolves, colts, goats, buffaloes, foxes etc. that have their own role to play.

The narrator of these folktales also knows the psyche of tribals, temple-priests, gardeners, potters, sweepers, carters, peasants, swindlers, thugs (cheater). Another significant fact about these folktales is regarding the female characters in them. Almost all the female characters are bold, wise and enterprising. They give a befitting challenge to their counterparts and come out as winners. The stories like 'Brave-Braver-Bravest', 'Gyani-Dhyani and Rambai', 'Kalavati versus Kamalapati', 'Dhanvati Redeems Husband', 'Chhailu, Chalti and Bhola' are some examples.

Folktales offer a lot of laughter and enjoyment to its readers. Apart from satire and sarcasm, the stories single out some characters. Even their names bring amusement and the listeners expect a lot of joy from these folktales. Baau, the Jester is just such a character. Stories like 'Baau, the Jester', 'Sweat-soaked Quilt', 'Long Bearded Woman', 'Unwanted Guest', 'The Quacks', 'Ramlu and Dhapaan' provoke laughter and joy. 'Ranga and Ranghar' and 'A Thug Became a Kotwal' are very peculiar stories, and worth enjoying because of the twist in the story.

Folktales, like grassroots, are evergreen and ever enjoyable, be they set in the locale of mountain tops, sea coasts, deserts or jungles or any other type of landscape, as long as there are human beings inhabiting these areas. Folktales adapt to their cultural, social and even political environment. Some of the folktales included in this work are political satires related to our present democratic form of government. These stories can be termed as neo folktales. Stories like 'Can A Bullock Deliver a Colt?', 'Badlu versus Aayaa Ram and Gaya Raam', 'A Buffalo Owner', are some examples of this kind.

The National Capital Region (NCR) has been a centre of political power in India for centuries. As a natural corollary to this fact court culture has been flourishing here for all these years. But its folk-culture drawn from the lives of its common people has been neglected because those who were in power needed only hewers of wood and drawers of water for themselves from the locals and not perpetrators of culture. Hence little has been done to showcase the folk culture of this region through folklore, especially folktales. This is perhaps for the first time that a humble attempt has been made to apprise India and the world at large about the folk heritage of the land of the Mahabharata.

The author started this project about thirty years back realising that the ever-expanding boundaries of the National Capital Region of India, are rapidly swallowing up the villages around it. Haryana and Western Uttar Pradesh are the most affected. The tillers, farmers and peasants from this region are becoming labourers in multi-national industries. Their way of life is undergoing a sea change. Their social values and culture are being permanently eclipsed by the so-called civilized city culture. Society has no time to interact with the younger generation of these people. Their dialects are disappearing. Their folk literature, folk culture and especially their folktales seem to be bidding their time before their final departure to their graves.

This work of collecting the data of the region's folktales may prove a time capsule for generations to come.

During the process of collection, the author selected folktales related to the religious practices prevalent in this region. They include fasts of the Hindus practised annually, background story about these fasts, weekly fasts, stories about Hindu gods and goddesses, such as Ganesha. These collections comprise 83 stories were published and these books were brought out between 1992 and 1996 by the publisher, for distribution and sale in Delhi. The book entitled *Folktales from Haryana*, published in 2004 (Shipra Publications), includes 20 stories, most of these are on birds and animals meant for school children. But the author was not satisfied with these works. He wanted to compile a set of stories representing social set-up and which is now evident before the readers through these folktales. Of course, the author still feels that others should join him to keep the pace on.

The author expresses his sincere gratitude and thanks to his elder sister Pheemo Devi and his peer group, who have related the stories in this volume to him, from time to time. My thanks are also due to my wife, Smt. Vimla Kaushik; Sh. M.P. Bhardwaj; and Sh. M.K. Jain who went through the manuscript time and again to improve its language but maintaining the regional flavour of language and correcting spelling errors.

C-605, Saraswati Vihar
Delhi-110034, India

(Dr.) J.N. Kaushik

1. A False-witness Family

Land disputes are very common in villages. The sufferers generally file a suit in a court of law to get justice. They engage lawyers to present their cases properly. Witnesses are also arranged in support of their cases. They are served and fed well to win their favour. They are treated as special guests. Special conveyance is arranged to make their travel up to the courts comfortable. They are visited a day before the hearing to confirm their presence in the village. Litigants grease their palm. If a person stands as a false-witness, his expectations are higher from his client.

Once a family of a village became notorious for standing as false witnesses. This family was always in demand. They learnt all tricks from ill-reputed lawyers from generation to generation. Sujaan was the head of this family. Even judges were helpless before him. Their merit for judgement was not justice but the statements of the witnesses, cooked up, false or untrue.

Sujaan's family had acquired riches through such notoreity. They donated some money in the name of religion to win God's favour in their next birth. Even the names of their ancestors were engraved on temple walls and at places of religious importance. Some hailed this family as philanthropists while others considered them as hypocrites. Some villagers would say—It is *Kaliyuga*. Falsehood thrives in this age. Some argued that justice might be delayed in His court but it is not denied. This family was bound to be'rewarded' with what was due to it.

Once a *sayana* or an astrologer came to that village. His forehead was painted with sandal paste mixed with many auspicious colours. His neck and chest were decorated with a rosary and other beads interwoven with multicoloured jewels and pearls. He wore a silken turban. His *achkan* and saffron *dhoti* suited his attractive personality. The news of the arrival of this *sayana* spread like wild fire in the village. The womenfolk were happy, as they could enquire after the evil spirits that haunted them and also ways to pacify them. He was to stay in the village temple. Special food was arranged for him. The temple priest was happy to see the villagers throng to his premises in the hope of meegting the *sayana*.The *sayana* in turn, guided and pacified many men and women. He solved many problems in his own religious ways.

Those were *Shraddh* days. The villagers were busy performing *Shraddha* rituals in honour and for the benefit of their deceased relatives. Some were offering *Pindas* to the spirits and gifts to Brahmans and to relatives.

Sujaan's family had also arranged *a Shraddh* ceremony. They invited the *sayana* to offer him a special *Shraddh* feast. When the *Shraddh* ceremony was over the *sayana* left for the temple.

It wasthe day of *Amavasya*, the last day of the *Shraddh* fortnight. People were free after offering *Pindas* even to their forgotten deceased relatives. In the afternoon they gathered in the temple courtyard to know the fate of their *Pitraas,* deceased relatives, from the *sayana.* He was believed to have special knowledge about *Pitriuloka,* where the ancestors supposedly live after death.

There were many questioners. The *sayana* was answering their queries. Sujaan was also present along with his family. He was in a boastful mood because he had donated clothes and cash to the Brahmans on that day. He wanted to know the fate of his ancestors. He was sure that they must be in heaven because they had made so many donations during their lifetime. Temple walls stood as testimony of their generosity because their names were written on donors' lists hung up on the temple walls. Sujaan even offered the *sayana* advance *dakshina,* the fee for religious service, for his services.

The *sayana* took out a slate and pencil from his bag to draw a horoscope for locating the position of souls of his ancestors. He checked the positions thrice to make sure of the exactness of their locations so as to to remove any doubt. But each time, the lines got blurred. He took out a holy manuscript having separate leaves tied together. He redrew the *Pitraas* horoscope.

By now sweat drops had begun to appear on the *sayana's* forehead. The sandal paste on the forehead had caked and begun to crumble. He kept nodding his head time and again. His eyes became red. He bit his lips. They felt dry. He ground his teeth. He bit his forefinger in astonishment. He looked towards the onlookers as if some evil souls were haunting him.

At last the *sayana* broke his silence. He turned towards Sujaan and said, "Your Pitraas are in Cow-dung loka. They are ill-fated. Don't ask more about them." The gathering was surprised.

Sujaan said imploringly, "Oh sir, I have heard about *swargya loka, or heaven, narak loka,or hell, paataal loka*, one of seven subterranean regions and other lokas during discourses. I have never heard about Cowdung loka. Please explain; please reveal the mystery.

"I can show this Loka to all of you. But you will be sorry to see it," said the *sayana*.

The gathering looked at each others' faces. Some of them became pale, some trembled, some murmured, some closed their eyes, while others felt non-plussed. Only one person was smiling.

Sujaan gathered himself together and said, "I am bold enough to face any reality. I never felt afraid before the judges in open courts. Please reveal the reality of Cowdung Loka, wherever it might exist.

The *sayana* pointed towards the cow-stall of the temple. There were cow-dung heaps piled there. Some crows were sitting on them. They were scratching the surface in search of food. The *sayana* asked Sujaan to bring a cow-dung lump and place it near him. Sujaan obeyed hesitantly.and brought it. The *sayana* turned it upside down. Many restless insects were crawling in it.

The *sayana* said, "Here are your ancestors. They must have committed some heinous sins. I do not know about your family background. The public can judge their actions. My horoscopic calculations are clear."

There were loud cries from the public, "This family is ill reputed as providers of false witnesses at court. They have ruined many families. The crows are enjoying a feast on the cow-dung piles and the insects in it that the crows are gorging on, are the dead ancestors God is righteous. He is just. He never spares evil doers. He has proved it in this open court during Shraddh days."

❄ ❄ ❄

2. Chiranjivi: The Temple Priest

Once there was a sadhu. His name was Chiranjivi, which means one gifted with a long life. The villagers called him Chiranji. He was a bachelor, and had a well-built body. He enjoyed feasts every day in one house or the other. His feast invitation was fixed in advance. Some families would wait even for weeks together to feed him.

Feeding him with rich feasts the vilagers believed ensured the best rebirth.

Chiranji was a good blend of various professions. He could prepare horoscopes by calculating movements of the planets at the time of a child's birth. He could calculate auspicious days for marriages, auspicious days for digging wells, while laying the foundation stone of the house or *grihpravesh* at auspicious times, were at his fingertips. You just had to ask him a question and his thumb would start jumping and dancing on his fingertips. Auspicious travelling days towards the East or West or South or North were rendered in simple verse. He would murmur the *sani-chandre tyajeit poorvam.* Villagers observed fasts and festival days as per his advice.

Those who were averse to astrology would bow before him for any type of cure—be it epilepsy, mumps, measles or ulcer, sore, or tumours of all types.. He ministered to his faithful bunch by uttering mantras and swishing a peacock-feather broom which any case has germicisdal properties. For the others he would hand out desi-medicines mixed with the ashes of various herbs and metals.Thus he had earned the reputation of one for whom no illness was incurable. He was virtually the *Charaka and Lugman* for the villagers.

Young wrestlers were always happy with Chiranji. There was a wrestling *Akhara* or arena in the village temple. Wrestlers of all age groups would assemble there early in the morning and in the afternoon, according to wrestling days and seasons. The temple well had good arrangements for their bath. Massage experts helped the wrestlers with body-building. Chiranji used to reward them. The village pond remained full during the rainy season but during the dry season it had to be filled with water from the village well. Wrestlers would swim across this pond from East to West ten to fifteen times as a part of their regular exercise routine. The problem with Chiranji was that he never had a chance to learn swimming. He could just splash his hands in water. He envied the swimmers.

He loved the village children. He would tell them fairy tales and other mythological stories. When he sang *chopaaies* from the Ramayana, children were spell bound. He used to arrange some sports competitions and gave away prizes to all participants.

Sometimes, Chiranji would go begging for alms before sunrise. He would call loudly *Alakh Niranjan* ie., give me alms in the name of God. The women of the village, busy grinding grain on theirs hand grinding *Chakkis* would come out with veiled faces and offer him handfuls of flour. They would pour the flour in the long bag hanging from his shoulder. He would jingle the discs of his long brass tongs as a sign of blessing and proceed to the next door. The flour thus collected would be given to visiting *sadhus*. A part of it would be fed to the village oxen.

Chiranji was fond of tree planting. The greenery of the temple was always looked fresh. There were *Brindavani Peepals*. Children would swing from these trees clutching the long tufts of aerial roots. The *Barh and Gular* trees bore sweet tasting berries that the children loved. Parrots, pigeons and sparrows would chirp, hop from branch to branch and enjoy the fruit. *Tulsi* bushes and other holy plants were watered every day by the women and devotees. Chiranji would pluck the leaves to prepare *desi* medicine.

The four walls of the temple were in a neglected shape and water from the fields would seep into the compound during the rainy season. Chiranji was very scared of water. He always considered floods to be a bad omen, not only for the villagers but for himself too. His horoscope suggested that his life may be washed away by floods. So his father had decided not to marry him, as marriage meant widowing an innocent girl.

Floods were very common in those days. The *Sahabi Nadi* could not be tamed during the rainy season. The rulers of Alwar and Rewari states, through which the river flowed, had tried their best to channelise its waters but had failed. In the previous year, most of the fields had been flooded by its waters. Their crops were washed away. The distraught villagers, in a bid to save their lives had turned to Chiranji for help.

Chriranji told the villagers to sacrifice a goat—*Bali ka Bakra-* in the name of Lord Indra, the god of rains. A healthy goat was purchased. Sacred thread was tied around its neck. A *Tilaka* was applied on its forehead. A red cloth was tied around its body as a coffin. Chiranji recited some *mantras* to please Indra and the river *Sahabi*. Some wrestlers from Baba's Akhara caught hold of the sacrificial beast by its horns and ears. The villagers shouted slogans. The wrestlers threw the beast in the water. It bleated in horror.

To the great relief of the villagers, the river waters began to recede. The cause of its receding is a mystery till date. Some attributed it to Chiranji's brilliance. Others said that God had heard the sacrificial beast's dying call. Elders assigned this miracle to Indra's grace. Others conjectured that it could be the result of the invocations of *Devi-*

devatas by the women and innocent children of the village. Atheists announced that the embankment of the river had been washed away upstream and the waters had spread to some other villages. Whatever may be the reason, Chiranji had the upper hand in saving the villagers from devastation. They raised slogans in his praise. The goat which had survivied through the receding floodwaters, was allowed to freely enter people's fields. It was considered as sacred as the village ox.

As a gesture of thanksgiving, Lali, the issueless widow of a rich *Baniya*, renovated the temple. The sculptor placed Lali's bust in one corner of the temple. To please her he placed a straw in her lap to show that she was not issueless. People praised the sculptor's idea.

Another devastating rain flooded the *Sahabi Nadi*. The Dahar, a low waterlogged marshy ground, in the south, began to get submerged. Soon the waters were nearing the village streets. The villagers performed *Yajna* and arranged casteless feasts to please the village deity and other *devi-Devatas,* on Chiranji's advice.Alas! no *Dharma-karma* bore fruit. The villagers asked Chiranji to suggest some way out.

Chiranji closed his eyes for concentration and said, "Yes, there is one remedy most suited to this occasion."

The villagers felt happy. "Please tell, please tell", they shouted in one voice. "We are ready to make any sacrifice to save our village."

Chiranji said, "The *Sahabi Nadi* needs one young man to be offered as sacrifice. Arrange it and I shall do the rest."

The villagers looked at one another's faces. They arranged a *Chabutra* Panchayat. They went from door to door to find a volunteer. Finally. a lame young man offered himself as he took his life to be useless. But Chiranji told them that the gods do not accept lame persons as sacrifice. He asked them to search out some healthy man.

Being unsuccessful in their attempt, one ill-famed fellow whispered in his friends' ears. His friend said, "He is indispensable for the village. Wrestlers, old and young, rich or poor, all like him. He has rendered selfless service for the village for many years. Who would like to accept this slur? He may curse the whole village. All of us will be doomed."

"But doom is approaching us in the form of a stormy flooded river. This doom is certain and that is mere illousion."

They whispered in one another's ears and reached a unanimous conclusion in desperation. They accompanied Chiranji in their *Dunda* or village boat. Khussi, the chief conspirator and atheist unceremoniously pushed Chiranji into the gushing waters. Hell fell upon Chiranji—the chosen human sacrifice. He was already scared of pond water. His horoscope maker had predicted a watery death for him. Khussi pushed back the oars of the boat and all returned safe to the river bank. The villagers on the bank were surprised to see the boat return without Chiranji.

Meanwhile the gushing river water tossed Chiranji up and down. He went under, into the flooded waters, time and again. He remembered God and asked forgiveness for his sins. Nothing was audible in the whistling breeze. Though he had never learnt how to swim still he splashed the water to save his life. Fortunately a floating wooden log struck against his belly. There is a saying that a sinking man clutches at a straw. But this was a log matching with his weight. He embraced it as if it was God's incarnation in the form of a wooden saviour. He heaved a sigh of relief. Slowly but steadily the log struck against some bushes. The water all around was just knee-deep. The earth underfoot felt marshy. Ultimately he managed to wade his way to the river bank. He touched the earth with reverence and thanked his stars. He thought that some good deeds of his previous lives must have helped him.

Chiranjivi, before leaving for the Himalyas, left a note of advice for the villagers,

Giving profitable advice,
Is not always wise,
In adverse rainy days,
It can prove you otherwise.

How long Chiranjivi lived in the Himalyas is anybody's guess..

❄ ❄ ❄

3. Seeing is Unbelieving

Akbar and Birbal generally indulged in arguments over controversial issues. Akbar tried to have the upper hand as he was the *Badshah*. But Birbal was blessed with an extraordinarily sharp intellect. It is believed that Saraswati, the goddess of knowledge, was pleased with him. Whenever he took a stand to prove something, the goddess would show him the right path. Hence, his success was always a certainty. Akbar had to cut a sorry figure time and again. Still Birbal was his nearest and dearest *Wazir*.

Once they were out on a hunt. Akbar came across several new events during the course of the hunt, which hecould not believe outright. He turned to Birbal and said, "Birbal, I am told that seeing is believing. In that case, an event, which we see with our own eyes, must be taken as true. It is believable. It cannot be wrong. Hence, in future I shall try to see the place of happening before giving my judgement. People will praise my sense of justice."

Birbal listened to Akbar. He kept quiet for some time. Akbar could not tolerate his silence as he wanted immediate approval of his conclusion. Akbar said, "Can't you say yes to an undisputed saying?"

Birbal said "You are not the final authority. All that glitters is not always gold. Our eyes can deceive us. They can mislead us. Sometimes we may be de ceived if we trust an eyewitness' judgement only."

"You are arguing unnecessarily," Replied the Emperor. "I do not want such a Wazir. You always go against my argument. Mind your ways in future," said Akbar.

Birbal said, "Badshah Salamat, I request you to keep cool. Impatience can lead to wrong judgement."

"But can you disprove the saying that seeing is believing?" argued Akbar.

"Seeing is always not believing," persisted Birbal.

"Can you prove it?" challenged Akbar.

"A mustard seed cannot sprout on the palm immediately. Grass cannot grow under one's feet. They take their natural course. They take their own time. I can prove my words at an appropriate time," Birbal said with confidence.

The argument cooled down and time passed on.

One day, Akbar had gone out for hunting. Birbal was in the palace. He was looking after palace arrangements. He was keenly watching the servants' movements. Akbar's bedroom was to be specially decorated because it was his marriage anniversary day. Comfortable linen, springy mattresses, and sink-in pillows had been arranged and sprayed with scent. The entire bedroom looked heavenly.

Akbar's dress assistant came to supervise the work. He gave the final touches to costumes, curtains and other hangings. He touched the silken bedding and wanted to have a first-hand feeling. He climbed upon the bed, pulled up the quilted blanket and covered his face. He was so fascinated by the scent that he fell sound asleep. Birbal was watching this from a secret nook. He was silent, mum, cool and calm.

The queen graced the chamber after some time. Seeing the sleeping figure on the bed she assumed that the Emperor had returned tired from the hunt and was taking a short nap. She decided to lie down as well. Manwhile, Birbal was standing on the doorstep in the guise of a faithful guard. When Akbar returned after the hunt, he found Birbal standing outside his bedroom. Birbal salaamed the Emperor and requested him not to enter the room.

Akbar felt offended. It was his wedding anniversary. The queen must have been waiting for him most anxiously. Who was Birbal to spoil his game? He was the most-unwanted man at that time. Birbal spread his arms across the door as if he was the master of the room and Akbar was Mr. Nothing.

Akbar said, "Birbal, enough is enough. Don't stand in my way. I shall tolerate no more".

Birbal said, "Inside the room there is much more than 'enough'. You will have to tolerate more than this."

"What, what"! Akbar said surprisingly. "Yes, yes", said Birbal, "The queen is sharing her bed with your dress assistant".

"Oh no, no. What is all this hell? Have you gone mad?" frowned Akbar.

"No Sir, I am very much in my senses. You seem to have gone mad. You are disbelieving me. You may go and see all this with your own eyes."

"Yes, yes," said Akbar.

"But you will enter the room on one condition. You will do no harm to any of them," cautioned Birbal.

"Only time will tell, said the agitated ruler.

"Yes, I agree. Now you can enter the room," Birbal said.

He gave way to Akbar and followed him like his natural shadow.

Akbar removed the quilted blanket. He was shocked to see his dress assistant sleeping soundly on the bedding.

Akbar pulled out his sword. His eyes were reddened. His lips were quivering. He was perspiring. He shouted "Oh you bastard!

How did you dare to enter the lion's den! Your only punishment is death with my own sword."

Akbar drew his sword to strike the culprit. Birbal came in between. He requested Akbar to put the sword back in its sheathe.

Akbar roared, "Seeing is believing. Can you tolerate such an incident with your wife?"

Hearing the word "wife" the queen tossed and turned in the bed. The loud conversation in the bed room made her suspicious. She threw back her quilt and got up from the bed. She noticed the sword in Akbar's hand, Birbal was standing by his side and the dress assistant was lying on the floor begging for his life with folded hands. She could not connect all these things.

Akbar turned towards her. He shouted, "I will kill you. You have slept with your dress assistant. You flirt .... ".

Birbal said "Be cool Badshh Salamat. The queen is innocent. What you are seeing is not worth believing."

"You too are siding with her. I smell a rat. It is something more than mere suspicion," said Akbar.

The queen recovered herself. She tried to know the reality.

The dress assistant said, "I deserve to be slain. I entered your bed just to have a first-hand feeling of comfort and fell asleep".

"Oh, it was you, not the king, who was sleeping here? I mistook you to be the king. All this while I had been sleeping on the other corner of the bed thinking the Emperofr had gone to bed tired after the hunt and me not wanting to disturb the king," the queen explained.

The dress assistant fell at the queen's feet and begged for capital punishment for himself.

Akbar rubbed his eyes. He put his forefingers to his ears as if to clear a blockage. He wanted to know whether what he saw and heard was untrue.

Birbal said imploringly, "Seeing is not always believing, Sir. I have proved it."

Akbar's anger cooled down to normal. Then onwards he remained more judicious.

❄ ❄ ❄

4. A Foster-Son and Cotton-Seed

Once there was a farmer. He was very hard working. He got up early in the morning and ploughed his fields till sunset. The members of his family were very co-operative.

He had a handsome son. He was very well built and healthy. He also helped his father in tilling the fields.

One day his father had gone to visit some relatives. His son, Raja, ploughed the fields in his absence. The rainy season was about to set in. Wise farmers, without caring about the scorching sun, had cntinued to plough their lands so that the earth could absorb more and more rainwater. They knew that the furrowed surface of the land would prevent the rainwater from flowing off their fields.

By evening Raja, the young man, was dead tired. To take rest he lay down on the clumps and clods of the fields. Soon he fell fast asleep. He was drenched in sweat. His feet were smeared with earth. His clothes were wet due to sweat and he looked dirty.

The king of the land, who was out hunting with his nobles, saw the young man. He was attracted by his looks and good health but took pity on his poor condition. He stopped his horse and said to his Diwan, "I want to help this young man. I want to free him from his poor wretched plight."

His Diwan said, "My Lord, a farmer's life is such. They are accustomed to working in such conditions. They bear heat and cold. Let us not spoil them by making their lives comfortable. Let tillers remain tillers. At the most, you can help them get a reasonable price for their produce."

The king's horse neighed. The young peasant's sleep was broken. He was surprised to see that the king of the land was standing before him along with his nobles. He paid respect to them.

The king was pleased. He said, " Young man, I want to adopt you as a foster son. You accompany me to my palace. I shall provide you all the facilities of life."

The young man felt happy. He went to the palace. The king provided him with a cushioned bed. He was given a silken quilt. Some servants were at his disposal. He was served with the best food.

By the next winter he wanted to change his quilt. He sent for the cotton-carder. He instructed him to card the cotton carefully and set the cotton layers properly. He was also instructed to see that all the cotton seeds had been removed from the cotton boll. The cotton carder was professionally skilled. He listened to all the instructions and left the place.

He went to the market and purchased long-stapled cotton. He made sure that no cotton seeds remained wrapped in the boll. He carded it in daylight to give the best fine finish. He handed it over to the young gentleman.

At night the young man covered his body with the newly made quilt. As he tossed and turned to change sides he became restless. He noted a red scar near his arm pit. His sleep was disturbed. He spent a very restless night.

Next day he called for the cotton carder. The cotton carderhoping that the gentleman would reward him for his skillful hard-work, came immediately. To his great surprise, when he bowed to pay him his respects, the young man kicked him. He hit him time and again.The carded felt wounded. When the young man was tired he stopped the beating. The cotton carder began to cry out in pain.

Incidentally the King had not visited his foster son since long. As he was passing that way, he came along, with his Diwan and nobles. He was shocked to hear the screams and shrieks inside his foster son's residence. He said to himself, "I do justice to all. I take full care of my subjects. I donate and distribute so many things among them. Why this cry? I will personally find out the truth."

The King peeped through the window. A poor man was lying on the ground. He was bleeding. His foster son was murmuring some words in anger and kicking him. He went inside along with his Diwan and nobles.

The King said to his fosterson, "Has this man insulted you?" Has he broken in your house for theft? Has he come to kill you? What is wrong with him?"

The foster son said, "He has not offended me in that way. He is a cotton carder. I asked him to make me a quilt. He did not perform his work carefully."

The foster son tore off a portion of the quilt and took out a small portion of cotton seed. He said, "This part of the cotton boll was not carded. It caused scars and irritation on my body. I had a sleepless night. This lazy man deserves punishment."

Then the Diwan spoketo the foster son, "Do you remember the day when you were sleeping on the lumps of earth in an open field in summer? The King felt pity on you and adopted you as his foster son. On that day I requested the king to leave you in that condition. Today this small portion of cotton seed is troubling you. You are punishing a poor craftsman just for nothing."

The king said "Diwan ji, now he is no more my foster son. He is a heartless cruel person. Ask him to leave my palace. I am sorry, I ignored your advice."

❄ ❄ ❄

5. A Sweeper and the Queen

Once there was a beautiful queen. Her name was Chandermukhi. Her complexion was as bright as the moon. She was also broadminded in her thoughts. Her approach towards her subjects was humanitarian. Her name and fame thus spread far and wide.

Biju, the sweeper, used to sweep her palace. One day he had a glimpse of the queen when she was in her dressing room. He was wonder struck by her beauty. He could not express his love towards the queen. Opening his mouth for expressing love meant inviting a crushing death upon himself. He suppressed his thoughts but under this mental pressure he fell ill. His health began to fail. He stopped going to sweep the palace.

Once the queen saw a lady sweeper sweeping the palace. Chandermukhi, noted it. She said to herself, "Where is that sweeper? Why has he sent a pregnant woman in his place? It is injustice to her."

The queen sent for the woman.. She enquired after the sweeper. The woman, Dhaapaan, kept mum. When the queen insisted time and again, she said, "He is ill. His health does not allow him to work."

"What is the cause of his illness? What type of illness is he suffering from? Why does he send you to sweep the palace in this critical condition? Speak ougt or I will punish him," said the Queen.

The woman Dhaapaan, returned home. She related the incident to her husband. She said, "The queen wanted to know the cause of your illness. Tell it to the queen. The queen is very angry. She does not want me to work in these critical days. She will punish you if you do not reveal the truth. Our whole family may suffer a crushing death".

Biju, the sweeper, was badly shaken. He guessed, "It is sure death on both sides. If I do not go she may punish me. If I express my devilish desire, all the members of my family will be crushed to death."

He tried his best to evade the volley of questions raised by his wife. Ultimately he put himself at the mercy of his fate and said, "Do you have the courage to convey a blunt truth to the queen?"

His wife said, "Truth is always blunt. She may accept it as she likes."

"Do you give me your word?" he enquired.

"Yes I do," she said.

Biju said, "Once I saw the queen in her dressing room. I was dazzled by her physical beauty. What a fool I am! But I am helpless. I do not want to invite death on my family. We will be pressed to death in the oil-seed mill."

Dhaapaan was non-plussed. She never expected that kind of behaviour from her husband. But facts had to be knowingly or unknowingly. There was no alternative. God was their only saviour.

Dhaapaan went to the palace well prepared for the doom. The queen noted her facial expressions. Dhaapaan stood up before the queen with curled tongue and folded hands. She looked towards the earth. She was barefooted. She scratched the glittering floor with her toe-nail as if the earth would cave her in. The queen provoked her to open her mouth. She put a straw in her mouth as if she was a meek cow not to be killed.

The queen assured her pardon for any guilt and said, "What is the wish of your husband?"

Dhaapaan said haltingly, "My husband has been attracted by your beauty. He is hiding his face. He wanted to have love with you."

It was too much for the queen. But she had granted pardon in advance. The queen said, "To start with I would like to dine with him. Ask him to console, compose and restore himself for a fortnight."

Dhaapaan returned home. She related the queen's desire to her husband. He was stunned. Desire is a different matter but facing the hard reality is totally otherwise. How would he face the queen? How could he dine with the queen? But during the fortnight he managed to educate himself to face all the situations.

The appointed day came. He took a bath with perfumed water. He put on his best clothes. He saw his face time and again in the mirror.

Biju, accompanied by his wife, reached the palace at the appointed date and time, for dinner. The queen welcomed him. Flowers seemed to fall from the queen's tongue as she spoke. Biju was overjoyed.

The dining table was arranged with a variety of dishes. The scent of freshly cooked white Basmati rice wafted in the air. There were varieties of *daals* and mixed vegetables. He was happy to spot the dish of black urad as well.

The queen started mixing the Basmati rice with the daals and vegetables before eating them. Biju noted this strange style of eating: white, black, yellow, red, green, all mixed together. He looked towards the queen. She read his mind and said, "Colours are decepitve. My mixed plate will give me the same taste. Contemplate on my words."

Biju came to his senses. Time and again he repeated to himself—colours are deceptive, colours are deceptive, colours are ....

❄ ❄ ❄

6. A Pitcher with Two Bellies

Once there lived a prince. His name was Shravana. His parents were blind. He was a dutiful son. He looked after his parents very dutifully. He was always at their beck and call. They lived a happy life.

Shravana Kumar was married to a beautiful girl. She belonged to a poor and miserly family. She had inherited some of her familhy's traits from her maternal side. Her behaviour was very cunning and funny. She felt happy playing tricks. On the other hand, Shravana was devoted to his work and he had no spare time to observe her behaviour and traits.

Sharvana, was very fond of *khir*—a dish of rice boiled in milk with sugar. Everyday she prepared *khir* and enjoyed it with her husband.

Her parents-in-law were blind. They lived in a separate hut. They spent most of their time in devotion to God. She served food to her parents-in-law in their hut.

She thought that the *khir* dish was a costly preparation and she had to arrange milk, rice and sugar for it daily. Her parents-in-laws were gluttons. They consumed the greater portion of the dish each day. The wife wanted a way out of this trouble.

First she planned to cook food in two earthen pots separately. In one pot she would cook *khir*,and in the other she would prepare *raabri. As the raabri* could be made from chhach it was a cheaper dish because it did not need milk, rice and sugar. Some barley flour was mixed in it. It needed a pinch of salt. Also *raabri,* the thickened sour-type soup was easy to cook. It would be very digestive also for the old toothless couple, she argued to herself.

But another thought troubled her mind. Cooking *khir* and *raabri* would take up double the amount of time and fuel And her husband might note her trick. He might smell the cooking fumes.

She planned to prepare an earthen pot with two bellies. In one part she would cook *khir* and in other *raabri* for her in-laws. She went to the potter and explained her plan of making a special cooking pot with two bellies. The potter was a good craftsman. He prepared the pot as per his customer's requirement.

Shravana's wife handled the cooking pot with care. Her plan was very successful. Her parents-in-law were served with sour *raabri* while she enjoyed *khir* with her husband.

One day she cooked food in that pot as usual and went to have a bath in the river. She could not return by lunch time as there was a large crowd at the temple due to a special festival. Sharavana was at home. His parents were hungry. They were waiting for lunch.

Shravana's father said, "O Shravana, it is lunch time. We are hungry. Your wife has gone to the temple. We cannot wait for her. You serve us our lunch."

Shravana said "Yes father, I am just arranging the dishes for you." He went to the kitchen. He searched out two plates. He searched out a big spoon. He filled the plates with *khir* and placed them before his parents. Just to judge the temperature of the *raabri* his father touched it with his finger. It was tolerably hot. He licked his fingers to judge its taste. It was sweet. He realised that it was a *khir* dish.

The blind father said, "O dear son, today it is *khir*. Is it some special festival day? Your wife serves us sour *raabri* every day."

Shravana said, "No father, today is just a routine day. My wife prepares *khir* every day. I take *khir* in her company. How can you say that you are served separate dis?. There is only one cooking pot in the kitchen. I think you are mistaken."

Shravana's mother supported his father and said "Can't we distinguish the taste of *khir* from *raabr?*. We are given sour *raabri* every day."

Shravana was enraged to hear that allegation. He said, "You blind people are blaming my wife. I shall not accept your words."

His parents said in one voice, "Dear son, why should we blame your wife? We are calling a spade a spade. *Khir* is *khir* and *raabri* is *raabri.".*

While they were still arguing the wife entered the house and said, "I am very sorry that I am late. I will serve food for your parents."

Shravana said, "I have served *khir* to them. They areaccusing you of serving them raabri in place of khir. Is it so? There is only one cooking pot. How can a pot discriminate? I will not believe this old blind couple."

Shravana's parents said, "Blaming food is a sinful act. We do not want to be sinners. We will not swallow our words."

Shravana's wife kept mum. He asked her thrice but no answer came from her. He became very angry. He took the earthen pot in his hand and threw it on the ground. He was surprised to see the *raabri* spread over the floor. It got mixed with the *khir.*

The khir was glossy, while the *raabri* was dull. It looked as if the *khir* represented truth and the *raabri* the untruth. The k*hir* was the soul and the r*aabri* the *Maya* to wrap it. Shravana's eyes were opened to the truth. He took his blind parents on a pilgrimage and left home forever. It became a proverbial story. People still say, "*Aik Haandi Mein Doo Pet Kare thei us Shravana ki raani ne*"—*Shravan's* wife had prepared a pot with two bellies (to deceive her parents-in-law).

❄ ❄ ❄

7. Samsu Teli

Samsu *Teli's* was a joint family. He used to extract oil from mustard seeds. His heavy crushing wooden-mill was a centre of attraction for village children. When his black bull went round and round the mill a sweet creaking sound kept the bull alert. Its eyes were covered with cloth. The *ghunghurus* tied around its neck with a rope jingled with sweet sound. Generally his grand son sat on the log to drive the bull.

In spare time during winter season, Samsu used to card cotton. Traditionally his family was well known for cotton-carding. He would weed out all the cotton seeds while carding. The string of his spinning bow was so sharp that it would spread cotton flakes into air up to the ceiling. He was skillful in striking small-round *mogri* or mallet on the string. Its sound of *tain-tain* could be heard from a long distance. People could imagine from this sound that Samsu was at his work.

His wife and daughter used to help him in stitching the quilt. The load of the seasonal work was so heavy that 10 to 15 stitched quilts were at their disposal every night. They never needed a quilt of their own. They could even spare them for their guests.

Once most of the members of his family had to go to attend a relative's marriage. They were to stay there for about a month. His elder son Mahmood, who helped him day and night, was also away. Even young children used to help him in spreading cotton on quilt covers, collecting cotton flakes, which flew away to the courtyard and also in folding and unfolding the covers etc. But in the absence of the family members he found himself lonely and helpless.

Those were wedding days in the village also. People were arranging quilts for the guests in advance. Samsu had to card cotton for long hours. Quilt covers were piling day by day in his work place. Some customers came to his shop. They were talking about the arrival of large number of cotton bales in the wholesale market.

Samsu heard their conversation. He was shocked to know that large number of cotton bales had arrived. How would he alone card so much cotton? If he did not complete the job in time his customers would get annoyed. Under the stress he fell ill.

A neighbour looked after him and tried to provide best treatment. But all his efforts were of no use. The villagers felt restless because they had no other alternative to prepare their fresh quilts. The village Sarpanch came to know about this fussy situation. He too enquired about Samsu's health. The Sarpanch went to the city and consulted a doctor. The doctor agreed to examine Samsu.

The city doctor came and checked him thoroughly. He could not trace any symptom of illness. He left the patient's room and tried to enquire about the circumstances of his illness.

Samsu's two customers, who were talking about the arrival of large number of cotton-bales in the wholesale cotton market came and gave full details about his family. The city doctor jumped to the conclusion. The doctor said, "Samsu will be alright, but you will have to help me. I shall talk about the whole-sale cotton market in Samsu's presence. All of you will say that due to unknown reason all the cotton bales have been reduced to ashes. There was heavy fire in the wholesale cotton market". They agreed to city-doctor's suggestion

They went to the Samsu's room and talked about fierce fire in the wholesale cotton market. Samsu turned his ears to them and said, "What about the cotton bales?".

The Sarpanch said, "They have been reduced to ashes. The traders will have to arrange for fresh stock. It may take about a month to restart their sale".

"A month? A month? A month? By that time my son Mahmood will be back after attending the marriage ceremony. O Allaha; O Allaha; O God Great Allaha;" Samsu smiled. He stood up from his cot. He went towards his cotton carding room murmuring, "Fire in the wholesales cotton market. All bales reduced to ashes. One month time at my disposal. Mahmood will return". He took his carding mallet and started his work.

The onlookers were surprised. They praised the doctor's trick and paid his fees. The city doctor returned the money saying, "Samsu is an honest worker. He is poor and needy. I have gained new knowledge by giving him first hand psychotherapy. My successful treatment is a big reward for me."

It is heard that Samsu lived a long life and served the villagers till partition days.

❄ ❄ ❄

8. A Backbiter Wolf

Once there lived a lion in the cave of a mountain. It wasan ideal place for hunting. There was a rivulet, shallow water flowed in it. Animals could drink water without any hazard. Very long grass tossed near it. Small and big animals were fascinated by this sight for hunting. At night all sorts of animals came there to quench their thirst. The lion could hunt an animal of its choice.

There also lived a cunning fox. It knew the whereabouts of the lion and felt safe and sound. It taught to its cubs some tricks for hunting.

Days passed on. Once a wolf came to this territory. It was attracted by this area and decided to settle there in some thorny bush. The fox raised objection to it for the safety of its cubs. The fox warned the wolf about lion's presence but the stubborn and haughty wolf resisted. The discord reached to its height and they decided to teach a bitter lesson to each other. They departed with bitterness to take revenge at an opportune time.

Once the lion sustained deep injury in its hindpaws during hunting encounter. It limped while walking. Hunting the preys became very difficult.

The wolf saw the lion in trouble. It wanted to befriend the lion to teach a lesson to the fox with its help. It moved stealthily towards the lion and paid its obeisance with due respect. It offered its services to the lion for bringing meat to save it from starving. The lion was highly pleased with its offer.

The wolf hunted for the lion. The news of the lion's illness was spread like a wild fire by the wolf. All animals, big and small, came to pay obeisance to the king of the jungle. Some of them even dragged some hunts so that the lion could tear it according to its natural habit and taste.

Some wise animals suggested some natural drugs to cure the wound. Some animals applied antiseptic ointments. Some dressed the wound with dressing to keep it away from the deadly flies. Despite all best possible treatment the wound remained unhealed. But the lion was highly pleased with the services of the animals. The lion ranked the wolf as number one. The wolf bloomed with joy and howled.

Taking revenge with the fox was still torturing its mind. It thought that proper time had come to arrange some booby trap for the fox.

Once, when the lion was alone and licking its wound to sooth it, the wolf said, "Sir, you are the king of this jungle, small and big animals right from rabbits to elephants have come to console you. Even some wounded Rhinoceros, Giraffes, Beers, Hippopotamuses, Stag's etc. could not resist from enquiring about your health. Other animals forget their enmity and bowed before you. But I noted that one obstinate and cunning animal was missing. It did not turn up though it knew that you are ill".

"Who is that disobedient and proud animal"? the lion said roaring.

"My Lord, My Lord.........", repeated the wolf. "Yes, Yes, do not hesitate. Reveal its name. It will get a befitting punishment. This is royal darbar", said the lion.

The wolf said, "It is a haughty, proud and most disobedient fox, sir."

The lion recalled the presence of all animals one by one but the fox was missing from its memory.

The lion roared and said, "let the fox be brought. It should be presented before me. Let the entire jungle be searched out".

The wolf was happy. It thought that the least punishment for the fox would be its death in the open royal court. My vow and dream for its punishment would be fulfilled. "Wolf" is a proverb and known for its cruelty. It grit and grind its teeth in wolfish way.

A team of haughty animals led by the wolf searched out shrubs, shady bushes and other sporty hide-outs. At last they spotted it on the bank of a pond drinking cool water. The fox was very suspicious. It immediately connected the threads of all events. It bowed before the wolf and said, "The lion must have called me. It needs my services. I am in search of some medicine to heal its wound. I have found it out. Please lead me to the den of our royal King".

The wolf was happy because it so easily offered itself for punishment. The fox surrounded by those haughty animals reached the lion's den. The fox gave a majestic salute before the lion. It begged pardon for not coming to ask for its health. It expressed its difficulty because it could not found a suitable treatment for the wounded paws.

The lion listened its appeal and said, "O, you are so much interested to find out some cure for my wounds. I was given an understanding by the wolf that you are a proud creature. I wanted to kill you. Please tell if you have some medicine for me. You are so wise and well-wisher. You are so benevolent. Please tell me the cure. I am so restless. I am writhing with pain." The lion licked its wound and showed it to the fox.

The fox licked the wound and said, "My Lord, the King of this jungle. Your wound is very deep. Its medicine is next to you. You take it and feel yourself cured immediately. The medicine, which I suggest, is very reliable. It is panacea".

The lion said, "The medicine is next to me? Is it so? Tell me, tell me. I am so anxious. Do not delay".

The fox thought that it was one opportune time to take revenge with the wolf. Strike when the iron is hot.

The fox said, "The fleshy left ankle of a wolf is the most reliable medicine for your cure".

The wolf was sitting next to the lion. It had gained flesh by sharing the left-out flesh brought by other animals as a present for the lion.

The lion said, "Saving and preserving one's body is a pious law of the nature. Moreover I am the King of this jungle. I will heal my wound".

The lion jumped upon the left ankle of the wolf and chewed it immediately. The wolf felt non-plussed.

The royal gathering dismissed. The poor wolf came out limping and bleeding. The fox taunted and said, "Never resort to backbiting in royal court. Sooner or later one would be punished for it. Now suffer throughout your life and repent for it."

The fox and the wolf gazed at each other and departed for their abodes.

❄ ❄ ❄

9. The Unwanted Guest

Once there lived a young man. His name was Firtanand. He was fond of travelling. He used to visit his relatives living at far off places. He would stay for eight to ten days in one house. He would enjoy feasts and partake of the best dishes during his stay.Besides, he always expected someone from the houseto attend to his needs all the time. He was a glutton and a talkative fellow. All the relatives and friends were fed up with his visits. They generally taunted him but he was shameless..

One of his friends was Chaturanand. He considered himself to be both cunning and funny. He could manipulate various situations to his advantage.

His wife's name was Chalti. She too was very clever and talkative. Her neighbours appreciated her jests, funny pranks and jokes. She was very charming. She was always wel over it. She would cover the *kheer* dish with silver leaf to make it look showy.

Firtanand used to visit Chaturanand and Chalti's house. He had the good fortune to enjoy feasts with them many a time.

One day, Firtanand suddenly arrived at their door unnanounced.. It was their wedding anniversary day. Chalti had prepared special *kheer* of her liking. Both of them were annoyed to see the unwanted and uninvited guest. Too much nearness breeds contempt. They wanted to avoid him at any cost and spend a free and undisturbed day together.

Chaturanand winked at Chalti as a sign telling her to go indoors.He also followed suit. They hatched a plan. They proposed that the two of them should start a a mock quarrel so that Firtanand may leave their house during the spate of that ary scene.

As planned, Chaturanand began shouting at Chalti. He hit his shoe on the ground time and again as if he was beating Chalti mercilessly. She also shouted at Chaturanand. Both of them came out from the room.

Chaturanand said, "You have destroyed my home by your spendthrift ways. I cannot tolerate it. You leave my house or I shall shoot you dead with my gun."

When Firtanand tried to pacify them he was also pushed off rudely.. The wordy quarrel went on for some time. Chaturanand pulled out a gun and pointed to Chalti's breast. It was too much for the guest. He left the house. Chalti also ran outside the courtyard. Chaturanand locked the house and ran after her. Both of them were soon out of sight, in a narrow lane.

Chaturanand and Chalti went to a tea stall and took tea. They laughed at each other's mock acting. For some time they sat under a shady tree and were lost in their old memories.

Lunch time was nearing. They felt hungry. Chalti wanted to enjoy the *kheer*. They decided to return home because by that time they were sure that their unwanted guest had left for some other house.

But Firtanand was an obstinate fellow. Besides the aroma of the kheer was too inviting for him. If Chalti was shrewd, Firtanand was no less a match for her. He managed to scale the wall of their house. He saw that the pot was full with *Kheer*. He ate and ate till it was empty. He hid himself under a cot and fell off to sleep.

The couple returned home to have their lunch. They unlocked the door. They were laughing at their cleverness. They laughed at Firtanand and cracked jokes agt his expense. Firtanand got up from the sleep and heard their jokes.

Chalti was saying:
"I am so clever a lady,
Our guest has never thought,
What an artificial quarrel
I proposed and bravely fought."
Chaturanand boasted:
" I am so clever a friend,
Our guest had never thought,
I tried to kill you with an artificial shot"
It was a challenge for Firtanand's wit. He chattered under the cot:
"I am so clever a guest,
You have never thought,
I ate up your *kheer*
And slept under your cot."

He came out and stood before them. He twirled his moustache boldly. The couple understood that Firtanand had heard their boast. All the three had a hearty laugh.

❄ ❄ ❄

10. Baau: the Jester

Baau was a jester who enjoyed both fame and ill fame for jesting. God had blessed him with the quality of repartee. He had a ready and quick answer for every problem. He was so quick-witted that people liked his company. His presence at marriage parties was a must. He would convey invitations to the invitees faithfully and win them over with his spicy words. The guests at marriage parties awaited his presence eagerly.

He was not well-built. In fact, his stature was below normal. He was not fed well due to poverty. His complexion was somewhat sallow. His moustache was always drooping. The colour of the moustache hairs had reddened due to over-smoking. Though he was not a keen hookah smoker but it was his duty to test each hookah (smoking device) before putting it before the his master's guests. He was so skillful in preparing a fresh smoke that he never failed to put in the exact quantity of tobacco into the receptacle and would light a the right quantity of dung-cakes in order to release a balanced smoking experience. People relished it to the last puff.

He not only jested through words but resorted to practical jokes when needed. Once an elderly man at the village had taunted, "Baau, you always enjoy feasts at others' cost. Why don't you invite villagers and give a feast at your home?"

Baau said humbly, "I am a poor person. I have to convey messages of birth, death and marriage parties. In return people just pay me the customary *seawa rupyaa*-one and a quarter rupee-only. I have to feed a large family. I live from hand to mouth."

The elder said, "Don't find excuses. Your entire family enjoys good fare at others' houses. They even take back the remaining food home and enjoy *laddoos* for days together."

Some other people of the hookah party supported the elder. It was too big a challenge for Baau. He said, "Wait for that auspicious day. I shall arrange a party that you would never forget. This party will be remembered by generations to come."

"For generations to come? Such a lavish party!, said a hookah baz laughingly.

"Yes Zamindar Sahibaan. It will be according to your status. I do not want to let you down. I know your position. I will give due respect to you," said Baau.

The members of the hookah party were so pleased at the prospect of that unique party that they shouted 'Baau Ki Jai, Baau Ki Jai'. Some of them were mocking him about his high sounding assurance. He decided to pay them back in the same coin. Love begets love and hatred begets hatred.

Baau implored, "Sahibaan—I shall need your assistance."

"Yes-Yes," laughed one of them. "You just ask and we will fulfill our commitment. After all, this is a sort of Panchayat. We shall not go back on our words."

Baau was pleased with their words. He was happy because his plot was working well. He would net in all of them most cunningly. Words expressed in jest are not taken seriously. He would make full use of this situation. They would never forget Baau. In future they would never dare to cut jokes at his expense.

Whenever the villagers reminded Baau about the feast he would say, "Let the village *purohit* return from *Ganga Snan,* the holy bath. He will fix some auspicious day for the feast." But in his mind Baau was planning a most cunning trick as was his habit.

Then one day, Baau announced publicly the day of the feast. It was one week before Dewali. One adult member from each family would join the feast. Everyone talked about Baau's generosity.

Baau decided to collect utensils, plates and pans - big and small—from each invitee. No one sensed his trick. He collected a huge number of utensils and went to the pawnbroker. He mortgaged them with a detailed mortgage deed. He assured the pawnbroker that he would pay off the mortgage money by the time of the *Diwali* festival.

He had collected a tidy sum of money from the mortgage. He arranged a special *halwaai* to prepare the best sweets for his invitees. On the appointed day there was great hustle and bustle in the village. Every invitee was happy.

By mid-day the guests started gathering at the *chaupal* compound—the venue fixed for the feast. Carpets were spread over the clean and sprinkled ground. Sweets were served over leaf-plates. Vegetables, curd, pickles, cucumber were also served. After all the preliminaries were over, the village *purohit* announced that the gathering sxhould start the feast in the name of God.

As a gesture Baau took a hand fan. He began to fan the guests. They felt cool and praised Baau for that grand party. The guests praised him time and again and especially his manner of moving the fan from row to row.

Baau publicly announced with folded hands:

"This party is yours.
You are enjoying your own share.
No credit to Baau,
His contribution is only the hand fan air."

The guests laughed. They praised Baau, the versifier, and also for versifying the feast. None of them understood the hidden message behind the verse.

Baau murmured to himself, "They will not blame me in future. I have publicly disowned this party. They have taken their own contribution through utensils. I am just an organizer. My contribution is only hand-fan air. I am innocent. I have answered their joke. This joke is practical, not oral. I shall see, come what may."

When Baau did not return the utensils as per his promise fhe villagers started storming his home. He replied with courtesy that he had pawned their utensils at Kashi Ram Pital Ram Company. "Go and pay off the mortgage, and take back your utensil." This news spread like wildfire. Baau has cheated the whole village. He should be called before village Panchayat.

The Panchayat held an emergency session. Baau was called to explain his ill-deed or ill-deal. Baau came with no remorse on his face. He was smiling. He said with folded hands, "Chaudhry Sabhibans, do you remember what I said when you expressed thanks to me for the party? I repeat the words for your kind attention:

"This party is yours,
You are enjoying your own share.
No credit to Baau,
His contribution is only the hand-fan air."

The gathering looked at one other. The village Panchayat delivered no judgement against him. Everybody went to Kasi Ram Pital Ram Company to pay off the mortgage money in return for the their utensils.

No villager dare to cut a joke with Baau in the future. His name and fame is generally quoted whenever someone makes a mention about practical jokes. May his soul take rest in heaven.

❄ ❄ ❄

11. The Head Tribesman's Judgement

Sisu was the head of his tribe. He was an elderly man. He spoke less and observed more. His eyes, nose and ears helped him in arriving at judgements. He was ever conscious. He was well-known for his sharp mind and quick judgements. In certain cases other tribesmen sought help from him from time to time.

In his early life he was caught while stealing a woman's shawl.. It was his first act of stealing. The woman arrived at his hut to complain about the theft.. His family members did not oblige her. They said, "This is his first act of stealing. If we return it, that would be a bad omen. We will pay the price but not give back the shawl."

He trained his younger generations the tricks of his tribal traits. He could tell the age of goats, sheep, deer by the shape of their horns. He could fix the price of lambs at the time of birth just by seeing the condition of the hair and flesh on the bones. He could smell the presence of victims. Forecasting about the season was his pet subject. He was a part and parcel of his environment. They were one with each other.

Sisu had developed his own code language for looting or sparing a passerby. If he pronounced "*Basudeva*" in a loud voice it was an indication that the passerby is to be looted. To the passerby "*Basudeva*" was God's name. To his tribesmen "*Basu*" meant *baa*ns or bamboo and *Deva* meant strike. Strike the man with a bamboo. He possesses money. If Sisu pronounced "*Narayana*" loudly to the passerby it meant God's name to the passerby and to his tribesmen it meant, 'he has nothing with him. Do not try to touch him. Let him go."

Before committing a burglary, Sisu would make a hole skillfully in the back wall of the house without producing a sound. He would not enter it directly. There was a possibility that someonemight be awake in the house. He may be standing by the wall and may strike his head. He would take a small black pot which resembled a head covered in black hair. He would hang it on the stick and insert it inside the hole. If it was left untouched, he knew is was safe for him to enter.

If someone had a watch dog he would deal with it safely. He would kill it before sunset so that no immediate arrangement for an alternate dog could be made. Then he would become a peanutseller. He would hang a bag on his shoulder. He would throw poisoned pieces of flesh in the hedge and plants. The house dog would be attracted to the meat. The death of the dog was certain by night. Sisu's rival would sleep forever.

There were fixed days and dates for burglary. Dark nights were most suited to his work. The eighth day of the lunar month is bright and dark nights were auspicious. These are the *Devi's* days. He worshipped *Devi* as the mother goddess of the dacoits. If successful in his mission he would arrange a feast on those days. If someone committed theft among the tribe Sisu would trace him out by his own tricks.

Once a sheep from his herd was stolen. It was butchered and enjoyed by his fellowmen. This was too much for Sisu. Who could be the culprit? The thief left no mark. It was an open challenge for him. He suspected more than a dozen people. But who was the real thief? How could he trace him out? That was the big question.

He called a meeting. He declared that he would spare the thief if he admitted his guilt. No one came forward.

He noted the behaviour of eight people. He segregated them. He asked his tribesmen to assemble near the anthills on the southern bank of the river, for a feast. This was a strange request. His sheep had been stolen, but still he was arranging a feast. They smelt a rat. But the fare at the feast was so delicious that their mouths began watering.

When the party was over Sisu announced, "These little ants will tell who is the thief of my sheep."

They were surprised to hear his call. How was it possible? Have they special eyes? Were they eye-witness to the theft? Can ants speak? Can they give a nod? Do they bite the person who had stolen the sheep? None of them knew anything about that mystery. The thief among the gathering became very suspicious.

In the mean time, Sisu called out eight persons from the tribe, by name. They came out of the gathering. Each one of them was asked to stand on a separate ant hole. He said, "Spit near the ant hole three times." All of them obeyed his orders. They spat thrice. He asked them not to move till his next orders.

They stood there for five minutes. As the saliva from their mouths was sweet the ants started coming out from the holes. In no time they gathered in large numbers. There was one hole with a lesser number of ants. They came and disappeared soon.

Sisu observed this minutely. He allowed seven persons to leave the ant hole. The eighth stood there outwardly cool but inwardly disturbed. He began to tremble. Sisu caught him by the neck and said, "Here is the thief of my pet sheep." The thief began to weep.

A person from the gathering wanted to know that mystery. Sisu said, "As he is the thief his mouth went dry out of fear. He could not spit properly. His spit was salty. So the ants came out and disappeared."

The thief admitted his guilt. Sisu, the tribal head, announced his judgement. He said, "As a least penalty I shall whip him ten times. He will give me ten sheep from his herd."

The young man obeyed. All praised Sisu's judgement in locating the thief and the punishment he had meted out.

❄ ❄ ❄

12. Hansa and the Sandal Trees

Once there was a thick jungle at the foot of the mountain lopess. There were evergreen trees. They were very shady. Their boughs and hollow trunks were the main shelters for birds. The trees bore fruit throughout the year. The leaves of some of the trees were very tasty. The jungle was filled with birds and animals from morning till evening.

Some species of birds had been living in that jungle from time immemorial. They knew each tree's usefulness and suitability during different seasons. The birds made their nests on safer trees. Whenever there was some danger from wild cats or other bids of prey, they would chirp together to show their unity against the attackers. Their chirping sound was a useful tool for threatening their enemy. Their young ones had also learnt these chirps.

It seemed that even the trees, creepers and herbs in that jungle had developed a special oneness with the birds. The branches would move and remove their leaves with a hissing sound as if they were attracting and inviting the birds to enjoy their fruits, perching on their swinging boughs. Some fruits would emit an attractive fragrance to show that they were most tasty and nutritious. Some would attract birds with their shining colours or shapes. If the birds or their chicks pecked at some full-blown flowers, half-open buds or unripe fruit they would not mind. Even the leaves would not mind the birds leaving excreta on them. They would just shake off the dirt resting on their leaves. If a hunter visited the area, the boughs and leaves would comecloser together to hide the birds and the hunter woud not be able to spot the birds. There was perfect harmony in the jungle. Their eco-management system was perfect. The birds would help in growing more trees in larger areas by carrying seeds in their excrement.

The mountains, rivulets and brooks helped the trees grow in large numbers. The mountains poured rain showers. The clouds would to kiss or toss the trees by descending from their heights. The trees would hold their branches straight upwards as a support as if touching the clouds.

Time passed on for years and years. But all days are never the same. Summer is followed by the rainy season. The rainy season hands over to the winter, when everything is frozen. The winter makes no exceptions. It freezes everything within sight.

Once there was scanty rain in the jungle for some years. The forests, birds and rivulets, bore the pain patiently in the hope that Lord Indra would bless them with rain in future. The trees began to dry up. Their leaves began to fall. They bore less fruit. The water in the rivulets was just sufficient for the birds and animals to survive. Migratory birds flew away because were seasonal and selfish visitors to the jungle. They were foreigners after all. The resident birds had no other alternative. And besides, why should they have extra-territorial linkages? They were for the jungle and the jungle was for them.

For wood contractors the dry spell was very favourable. The birdsdisliked their presence in the jungle and would show their resentment by hovering around them, pecking their heads or by spoiling their food. The contractors snared some birds but the rest of the birds they did not leave the jungle.

Misfortune never comes alone. It is followed by bad to worse conditions. The outside settlers were not in tune with the jungle environment. A great wild fire broke out in the jungle due to their carelessness. . Piles of wood that they had cut down were engulfed by the fire. The contractors fled from the jungle because their selfish motive was limited to cutting down the jungle and not taking care of it. They wanted to save their lives.

Strong winds began to blow accompanied by a duststorm. It further stoked the flames and some of the dry trees were gutted to the ground.. The parched trees cried out in horror.It looked as if it was a night ofutter desolation.. Nothing would be spared.

But amidst all that devastating scene the grove of sandalwood trees was still saf. Although the trees could feel the heat of the forest fire,they were not in the immediate path of the flames. A whispering noise was audible amidst the cracking, splitting, bursting and exploding sounds of bamboos.

The Hansa bird family was sitting on the branches of the sandalwood trees. They too, were feeling the heat of the flames. They felt restless and kept hopping from branch to branch, but they did not fly away.

The fire was drawing closer to the sandalwood grove by this time. A sandalwood tree tried to urgee the Hansa family to fly away to safer places as they were blessed with beautiful wings. But the Hansa lot were a loyal breed of birds who felt sympathy for the trees because their generations have enjoyed a happy life on them. The sandalwood trees had never objected when they had plucked their flowers and fruit. They has spoilt their leaves but hey had tolerated every bit of this behaviour. The Hansa family could never imagine a life without these trees.

Lord Indra, the god of the rains, was highly pleased with the loyalty of the Hansa birds towards the sandalwood trees. His sympathy for the birds burst forth in the form of heavy rains. The fire started receding and finall, it came toan end. The Hansas and the sandalwood trees felt happy. It looked as if they were embracing each other.

A poet observed all that drama with his own eyes. He summarised the story in the following words.

O winged Hansas leave us and fly,
We rooted sandalwood trees, are to burn and die.
The Hansas said,
We enjoyed your fruit, shelter and flowers.
Burning together is the need of the hour.
Lord Indra was pleased and burst into shower,
Sincerity towards each other is a great power.

❄ ❄ ❄

13. Teku the Swindler

There was a *Thug* or swindler. His name was Teku. He thrived by his art of thugging or cheating. He could disguise himself as he needed to. He could speak in different tones. He could walk in different postures. Apart from a knowledge of various dialects he had also developed a secret or symbolic language. He had initiated his two sons into his art of thugging. They chose special occasions like fairs and festivals for cheating innocent people. Unfavourable times were a boon for them.

Once a drought had struck for some years. Due to lack of rain there was scarcity of fodder for the animals. People were disposing off their animals to butchers at throwaway prices.

Molar was a small marginal farmer. He was very fond of keeping a good breed of animals. His bullocks and cows won prizes at competitions. But he was badly hit by the drought that year. He had not considered disposing off his loving animals, but this time he found himself in great difficulty. He decided to sell his one bullock at the animal fair.

He got up early in the morning. He fed his bullock to its full. He caressed its body time and again to console himself. The bullock also felt the warmth of his affection and expressed its satisfaction by swishing its tail.

He left for the animal fair before sunrise. The fair venue, Jahajgarh, was nearly ten miles away. He wanted to cover this journey in the early hours to avoid the heat of the sun.

Molar had barely gone two miles from his village singing and humming, when a young man wished him. Molar responded. The young man offered to accompany him to the fair. They soon struck up a conversation. Seeing an opportune moment the young man enquired, "Are you going to sell this Dhandha (old bullock) at the animal-fair?"

"Dhandha, an old bullock?" reacted Molar sharply. "This animal is quite young. It has won prizes in competitions. Due to the drought I could not feed it well this year. This is not Dhandha—old bullock."

The young man said, "Old is old. I can buy it from you for the price of an old bullock. Give it to some butcher if you want more."

The young man's words stung Molar to the quick. But he swallowed his anger patiently as it was morning time and he had fallen on adverse days.

Molar marched on; the young man followed him. They came across another young man. He offered to buy the 'old bullock'. He repeated the same words as uttered by the former. Molar was again shocked. He again spread his hand softly across his animal, right from tail to head to reassure himself. He patted its back and it reacted like a young animal.. Molar felt confident.

All of them marched on, as their destination was Jahajgarh. They had hardly covered half of their way when another young man crossed their way. He said, "Who is the owner of this old bullock? Does he want to sell it? Why go all the way to the fair? Decide the case here and now. Only butchers will purchase it there."

The two young men pointed towards Molar. Molar soothed his bullock once again. He felt all signs of a young bullock in it.

All the three young men said, "An old bullock cannot be young just because you repeat it a hundred times. Let us decide the case through some Panchayat. The Panchayat would fix the price. Do you agree?"

Molar had full faith in a Panchayat. He gave them his word. They had hardly gone some miles when they saw five people sitting under a neem tree. They were smoking a *hookah* or hubble bubble.

Molar tied his bullock to a *neem* tree. The men in the panchayat talked about the prevailing selling prices of animals at the fair. They confirmed that the farmers were selling them at very low prices. There were no buyers due to scarcity of fodder except for some butchers from a nearby township.

Teku, the swindler, who had turned Sarpanch of this wayside Panchayat, said, "Who is the owner of this bullock? Is this old bullock worth selling at the fair?"

Molar heard the word "old bullock" time and again. He was so confused that he accepted their verdict as certainty and tried to dispose off the bullock then and there. He said to the Sarpanch, "You are an elderly man. You are the Sarpanch also. You decide the price of this bullock. From my side its price is five hundred rupees. I give you my word that I will accept the price fixed by you."

All of them were amused. They were happy at having successfully played their trick of trapping Molar into selling off his animal. The Sarpanch spread his hand over the body of the bullock. He patted its back thrice and said, "Its exact cost in these drought days is two-and-a-half rupees."

Molar felt as if a snake had bitten him, on hearing Teku's words. The Sarpanch for him was like a two-headed snake. Molar lost his stake. He handed over the ownership rope of the bullock to Teku. He looked in his face. He gazed at the big black mole, the sign of sin, on his face. He also noted that Teku had some knee problem.

Molar realized that he had been cheated by swindlers. He decided to pay them back in the same coin and to get back the full price for his young bullock.

Next day, Molar disguised himself as a hakim and a knee specialist. He went to the street where Teku lived and announced in a loud voice, "Is there someone with a knee problem? I shall cure him with full guarantee. I will return the money if the disease reappears". Teku looked out through his window. Molar noted the big black mole on his face. Teku was alone. His three sons were out in the fields. He came out with a limping leg. Molar asked him to go inside and lie down on his cot.

As Teku entered his house the *Hak*im bolted the door from inside. He gave merciless kicks to the swindler Teku and said, "Was my bullock worth two-and-a-half rupees? Take out the money or I shall teach you more lessons."

Teku felt helpless. He paid two hundred rupees to *Hakimji.* but his inner revenge was not satisfied. Next day he disguised himself as a *Vaidya.* He went to Teku's street and announced, "Is there anyone suffering from back pain? I shall treat patients without charging money."

Teku took *Vaidyaji* as a messenger sent by God to him. He asked his son to call in the *Vaidyaji. Vaidyaji* knew the points where he had hit hard yesterday. He located them at the first touch. *Vaidyaji* wrote a prescription for medicines and asked Teku's son to purchase them from some nearby township.

As Teku's son left the house *Vaidyaji* bolted the door and said, "Was my bullock worth two-and-a-half rupees? Take out the money or ...."

Teku took out two hundred rupees from the fold of his *dhoti. Vaidyaji* left for his house. Teku related the matter to his son when he returned with the prescribed medicines.

Molar said to himself, "Teku, the swindler, still owes one hundred rupees to me. I must charge this amount from him." He cooked up a plan. He dressed himself as a *pahalwaan* or wrestler. Some children were playing in the street. He distributed sweets among them. He said, "I shall give special sweets to the one who would go to Teku's house and shout out loudly, before running away, "Was my bullock worth two-and-a-half rupees?"

Some children agreed. They repeated the words as told by Molar, the *pahalwan.* Teku said to his sons, "Today Molar has come with his friends. Catch them all. All the three sons ran after them in different directions.

Molar jumped the wall and caught Teku by the neck. He said, "Rupees one hundred are still due from you as the actual bullock price. Return the amount and I shall free you from my clutches forever."

Teku gave him one hundred rupees and asked for forgiveness. He gave his word that he would never cheat anyone in future.

❄ ❄ ❄

14. A Hookah Addict and Yamadutas

Shera was a *hookah* addict. His father was a hookah smoker. Right from his early age Shera used to change the water of his father's hookah thrice a day to make it fresh. Shera had to smoke it time and again to ensure that it is properly set from all point of view. His father gained respect through hookah because he used a special type of tobacco-*karuwa tamaku.*

Through hookah he came in contact with various type of people—good and bad. But bad characters overpowered him in all sorts of behaviour. He would never hesitate in committing evil deeds. He rather enjoyed when his plan met with a success.

When his father died he was the full owner of his house. He became a chain hookah smoker. He indulged in undesirable acts. Elders warned him. They warned him about his life after death, about the punishments and torments to be inflicted by the messengers of Yama and the like.

Shera was bold. He never thought that he would be attacked by unheard of diseases and bodily pains. He looked old at an early age. At last he was on his death bed.

Lord Yama's messengers knocked his body. They took out his soul. Shera's self said, "Gentlemen who are you? Why have you come? Where will you take me? What arrangements you have made for my safe journey?"

The messengers never faced such an arrogant man. But they were all powerful. One of the messengers said, "We are Lord Yama's messengers. We have come here to take you to *Yama loka*. We will present you before our Lord of Death, Yama. He will give his own judgement according to the deeds done by you. We have special *Yama passa* or rope to tie you. You are safe in our hands till you are handed over to *Lord Yama* in his court."

Shera realised that he was helpless before them. He found himself automatically in *Yama passa*. Shera was very talkative. He indulged in talks to misguide them.

He said, "I have heard that there are many *Lokas—Swarga*, *Narka*, *Patala* and others. What path will you take?"

One of the Yama's messengers said, "We have just received a message that you are to be thrown in *Narakaloka*—the hell. Your deed scroll reveals that you have never done any good deed. Good doers deserve *Swargaloka*. You will be thrown in boiling oil pans". They told him about other horrors of *Narakaloka*.

"Shera did not lose his presence of mind. He still wanted to befool them. Shera said, Which *Loka* are we passing through"?

A messenger said, "We are passing through *Swargaloka*. See that gate in-front of you. That is the indicator of the beginning of *Swaga* territory.

"O *Swaga* territory? So near is *Swarga* territory". Shera said, "I honour your Lords judgement for sending me to *Narakoloka*. I bow before his judgement. He is the Lord of Justice. Take me to *Narkaloka* but ....".

"No ifs and buts", said a messenger.

Shera mustered courage and said, "I have a last wish. Last wish of a departing soul is honoured on our earth by the judges. You belong to Yama's court. You are supposed to be very kind and considerate. Will you please listen to me".

Shera used very flowery and flattering language as he was versed in entrapping his victim on earth. The messengers were flattered by his oily tongue.

The head of the messengers team said, "Though your deeds are other-wise than the language you use, yet we feel pity on you. We will fulfil your desire. But it should not be at the cost of our service and life".

Shera bowed before them and paid *Sashtaang Pranaam*—made with eight parts of the body (forehead, breast, shoulders, hands and feet)—touching the earth. Their hearts were melted.

Seeing most appropriate moments Shera said, "I just want to have a look at *Swarga loka*. You have some local powers with you. Use them. I will return immediately after having a look. Please untie my hands and feet".

The messengers were so much impressed by his words and behaviour that they untied the *Yamapassa*. Shera jumped inside the Heaven-gate and disappeared. The messengers were nonplussed. They felt that they have invited their own death at Yama's hands. They should have not believed a man from earth.

They tried to find out some solution. They rolled and unrolled Shera's deed-scroll time and again to find out his tastes and distastes.

They noted that Shera was most fond of smoking hookah. He had a special taste for *Karva—Tamaku*. By their special skill they immediately arranged a hookah and prepared it afresh with *Karva-Tamaku*. They disguised themselves as hookah-smokers.

They inhaled and exhaled hookah smoke and blew it towards Heaven's gate. In no time the environment was permeated with *karva-Tamaku* smoke. Shera smelt it. He was surprised to enjoy that smell. He thought that hookha smokers live in heaven also. He was attracted by smoke and searched it out just as bees reach juicy and fragrant flowers.

He noted three rustics smoking a hookah. He wished them good morning and said, "Will you kindly allow me to smoke with you? Please tell me your caste so that I may join a caste hookah".

One of the smokers said, "We belong to your caste. We recognize you. Come and enjoy *Karwa-Tamabu*."

He was overjoyed. He caught hookah's handle with his fist. The messengers tied his hand with *Yamapassa*. Shera realised the reality. He was again in fitters. He had to pay the price for hookah addiction.

❄ ❄ ❄

15. A Thug became Kotwal

Once there was a King. He was very proud. He always claimed that no *thug* or an imposter could cheat in his kingdom. He called himself as *Dedh Chhail* which mean that he was one and a half times greater than his challenger in all respect.

Once a *thug* heard about *Dedh Chhail's* challenge. This cheat was proud of his art of thuging. He was a big imposter. He called himself as *Adhai Chhail,* which mean that he was two and a half times greater than his challenger.

Adhai Chhail, the thug, sent a message to *Dedh Chhail* that he would come to cheat him and his public. The king should accept his challenge. If the king was *Dedh Chhail* he was *Adhai Chhail.* He would always prevail upon the king and his officers.

When the king received this challenge he called his Ministers, *Kotwal* and *Faujdar*. He warned them to be very attentive. If something untoward happens he would suspend them. The king proclaimed this message publicly by the beat of drum from street to street. Public became curious, cautious and conscious. The King was satisfied after this proclamation which was well received by his public.

The *thug* came to the King's kingdom to throw his trump. He decided to throw his trump upon trump till he was a final winner to lift his trophy. The *thug* sent his entry message to the King. The spies informed the King. The King called his *kotwal* and *faujdar*. He warned them to be extra cautious.

The *Kotwal* rode on his horse as a beat officer. At the dead of night he heard a noise of a hand grinding mill in a shattered building. A old woman, in tattered dress, was grinding a *chakki*. She looked tired. The *Kotwal* said, "Why are you grinding *chakki* by mid-night? You are so old. Do not the members of your family feel pity on you? You are in tattered dress."

The old woman said, "*Adhai Chhail,* the *thug*, has ordered me to grind *daal* for his horse. He would come after looting the King's palace. I shall grind by that time."

The *Kotwal* felt happy and amused. He said to the old woman, "I shall grind *chakki* in your place. I shall wear your dress. You go to your home, I shall arrest him when he returns."

The lady thanked *Kotwal*. They exchanged their dress. The *thug* went to *Kotwal's* house and looted it at his convenience. The *Kotwal* continued grinding the *chakki*. The *thug* did not return by sun-rise. Some recognised the *Kotwal*. *Kotwal* was ashamed. *Kotwal* returned to his house in bad shape. His wife told him that some one came here in *Kotwal's* dress. He looted our house".

The news of ransacking and looting of *Kotwal's* house spread like a wild fire. The King heard this news. He called *Kotwal* to his palace. *Kotwal* related whole real happening to the King. The King could not believe his ears. He said to himself, "If I am *Dedh* he seems to be *Adhai*. But I shall see him myself. Let time tell". He dismissed *Kotwal* from his service because he could not protect his own house. *Kotwal* was helpless. He had no excuse to offer.

Next day the King asked his *Fauzdar* to be more vigilant to catch the *thug*. *Fauzdar* rode on his horse and went from street to street. He noticed a beggar in one corner of the street. *Fauzdar* thought, if he could exchange his dress the thug would take me as beggar. He could catch him in beggar's disguise. The beggar obliged him happily. The *Fauzdar* roamed from door to door. The *thug* entered *Fauzdar's* house and had his free hand in looting. He kicked the horse with his booty and left the horse in the jungle. The horse returned to his master's house most faithfully. *Fauzdar's* wife was surprised to see the horse without his master.

As the daylight became clearer *Fauzdar* was disappointed. People saw *Fauzdar* in a beggar's dress. He was ashamed. When he reached his house he was shocked to know that his house has been looted by someone in *Fauzdar's* dress. He struck his head against the wall. When the King came to know that the *thug* had looted *Fauzdar's* house he dismissed him for his utter failure in his duties.

Next day the King decided to searchout the *thug* himself. He too rode on his horse. As the night fell the King noticed an old woman on a cross-road. She was worshipping some black idol and muttering some strange songs. The King said, "What is the trouble with you?"

The old woman said, "I am an issueless woman. My elder and younger brothers-in-law's wives tease and curse me. I am worshipping God. He may bless me with some issue". The King felt pity on her.

The old woman said, "O horse-man, why this small wooden box with you? Are you some magician?".

The King laughed and said, "I am King. My name is *Dedh Chhail.* I want to arrest *Dhai chhal*, a big *thug*. If I catch him I shall entrap him in this wooden box".

The old lady said curiously, "O King, how can a man be shut in it? It is so small".

The King said, "I can show you how a man can be forced to sit in it." The King jumped inside the wooden box. The old woman immediately bolted the box from above. The King was trapped and remained there till sun rose in the sky. The *thug* looted King's palace and fled away with the booty.

When the King did not return to the palace till late morning, some spies went out in search of him. They suspected some foul play done by the *thug*. One of the spies heard some wailing noise inside the wooden box. They broke it open. They were surprised to see that king *Dedh Chhail* jumped out of it.

The King was angry. He shouted, "Where is that old lady who bolted this box"? A spy said, "He must be that *thug*". The King scratched his head and said, "Yes he must be *Adhai Chhail*". When King reached his palace he was shocked to hear that the *thug* has robbed his palace. The King publically accepted, "If I am *Dedh Chhail* he is *Adhai Chhail*. He is more wiser than the King".

The King decided to make the *thug* his *Kotwal*. He was sure that if the services of such a person could be harnessed properly he could prove a best person for the kingdom.

The King announced publicly that he wanted to make *Adhai Chhail* his *Kotwal*. His crimes of cheating and looting were forgiven. He would come to his *durbar* without any hesitation and reservation. All appreciated his wisdom.

When *Adhai Chhail* heard this announcement he thanked his stars. He appeared before the King with folded hands and said, "I have no ill-will towards anybody. I accepted King *Dedh Chhail's* challenge. No one can claim that he is the wise person in the society. He bowed before the King and accepted the *Kotwal's* post. It is heard that there was no robbery and cheating case in the kingdom till the new *Kotwal* decorated that post.

❄ ❄ ❄

16. The Quacks

Once there was an old man. He was very wise. He was a good observer. He used to treat the patients. Some people called him *Vaidyaji* and others as *Hakeem* but generally he was called *Doctor Sahib*. He learnt some prescriptions from his ancestors.

Vaidyaji had a well built body. All the villagers took his shelter for treatment. He had some ready made medicines from local herbs. He was assisted by some *Chelas* or disciples.

As he was growing older and older he was in search of some good *chella* or disciple. He picked up some youngmen to initiate them in to his profession. They used to accompany him on his visits to the patients as a part of training.

One day *Vaidyaji* visited a patient. He entered the house. He looked here and there and went to the patient's cot. He had covered his face. He was suffering from stomach pain. *Vaidyaji* held his hand to feel the pulse. He felt the pulse of both the hands turn by turn. He put his palm on his belly and struck it with fingers. It produced a strange echo. The patient started hiccuping.

Vaidyaji pulled his face and said, "Has he taken *Sitaphal* or sweet pumpkin. Sweet pumpkin produces air in the stomach. Hiccups and inflated stomach are its clear symptoms".

His family members were surprised at *Vaidyaji's* findings. Actually they had grown *Sitaphal* in their fields and used this vegetable daily. *Vaidyaji* prescribed a *churan* or a digestive powder. They collected it from his home. The patient became normal within two hours. His wife came to *Vaidyaji* with some gifts like *gur* etc. as a good gesture. *Vaidyaji* blessed her and gave some instructions as per habit.

One of his *chelas* said, "*Vaidyaji*, how did you came to know that the patient had taken *Sitaphal*. Please guide me? If you are not available to the villagers I could help them."

Vaidyaji smiled and said, "Apply your commonsense. When I entered the patient's house I noted that some peels of *Sitaphal* were scattered in one corner. Husks, peels or rinds scattered in the house tell me the story. Patient's surroundings help in locating these signs and symptoms".

His *Chela* was happy. He was always in search of an opportunity when his *guru*, the *Vaidyaji* would be out of station and he would apply his prescription.

Vaidyaji used to go to *Ganga*ji to take holy bath. One day *Vaidyaji* was out of station. An elderly man fell ill. His family members searched *Vaidyaji* but they were disappointed as he was away to *Gangaji*. One of his disciples offered his services for examining the patient. The old man's son agreed hesitatingly.

The *chela* entered the patient's house. He looked here and there to locate some signs and symptoms connected with the ailment. He felt his pulse time and again. He stuck his stomach with his finger in line with his *guru's* footings.

He said to the old man's son, "Your father has swallowed the horse".

"Swallowed the horse?" The old man's son reacted immediately "How he can swallow the horse"!

The *chela* said, "I noted the saddle in one corner of your house. The horse is missing. He must have swallowed the horse. My treatment is exactly on the lines of my *guru*. Say yes to my question".

His son became angry. He pushed him out from his house. The *chela* had to cut a sorry figure. The old man's son related the matter to *Vaidyaji* when he returned from *Ganga Snan*. *Vaidyaji* had a hearty laugh on his *Chela's* foolishness. He sighed and said, "What a under cooked *Chela*. He will earn bad name for me. Better to oust him from my house".

Once a camel fell ill. It had some breathing problem. Its long neck was choked. It began to struggle for breath. The owner of the camel searched out *Vaidyaji* in some nearby village. The *Vaidya* crossed the desert area and reached his cottage with one of his *Chelas.* The Camel was restless. It was writhing with pain.

Vaidyaji touched its neck with his soft hand and noted some blockage in the mid of its neck. The *Vaidya* said, "Did it go to the desert land for grazing? Did it swallow some cucumbers?"

The owner of the camel said, "Yes Vaidya ji. You have rightly located the problem. Yesterday it ate cucumbers".

The Vaidya asked them to bring a brick. He hit the blockage part of the neck with the brick. The cucumber inside the neck was crushed. The camel started breathing in normal way. The Vaidya, *Chela* and the owner of the camel were happy.

Once again *Vaidyaji* had gone for *Ganga snan.* An old lady was asthma patient. She developed serious breathing problem. She began to convulse in her cot. She was gasping. Her son went out to call *Vaidyaji.* One of his *chela* was available. Old woman's son told him about her breathing problem. The *chela* felt happy because his *guruji* had treated a camel suffering from breathing problem. The *chela* had noted his treatment. The *chela* agreed to accompany him.

The *chela* touched the old lady's neck. He said, "Did she went out to desert land?" His son said, "No".

The *chela* insisted, "Say yes" as customary word. These are my *guru's* instructions. The son said, "Yes", as customary word. The *chela* asked him to bring a brick. He handed over a brick to the *chela.* The *chela* hit the oldwoman's neck with that brick. The old woman was already having breathing trouble. She stopped breathing. Her eyes turned upward. She became motionless. The chela noted it and said, "She has been relieved of her pain. My treatment is successful".

The old woman's son became furious. He tried to hit him. But the *chela* sensed the trouble. He ran out from the house. The young man followed him but he disappeared in darkness. The *chela* was never seen again. When *Vaidyaji* returned and came to know about the story he felt sorry.

One day *Vaidyaji* was going to a nearby village with a *chela* in hot summer. He saw a well under a tree and took rest. He saw a grass cutter coming towards him. He had a *kurrpi,* a flat bladed grass cutting tool, in his hand. He said to *Vaidyaji,* "My *khurpi* is suffering from high temperature. It is so hot that I cannot touch its blade. Please treat it immediately so that I could use it".

Vaidyaji smiled on his foolishness. But the customer was to be satisfied. He said, "Tie your *khurpi* with a rope and dip it time and again in the well".

The grass cutter followed *Vaidyaji's* instruction. He tied the *khurpi* with long rope. Dipped it time and again. When he pulled it out it was cold. The grass cutter felt happy. He thanked *Vaidyaji* and went for his work. The *chela* was happy to learn new type of treatment.

Once *Vaidyaji* was out of station. An old woman was suffering from high fever. The new *chela* was available in his place.

He went to the old woman's house. He felt her pulse. The fever was high. He asked for a long rope. He tied it with the old woman's neck. Her sons dipped her in the well of the house time and again as instructed by the new *chela*. When she was pulled back *Vaidyaji* felt her pulse. She was cold in all respect. The *chela* asked them to give her full rest for some time.

After some time they removed her shawl. They found her completely dead. They searched out the *chela* to give him deserving treatment but he had gone to other assignment.

When *Vaidyaji* returned he came to know about the old woman's death. He felt sorry. He decided not to initiate new *chela* in to his profession because all of them proved quacks.

❄ ❄ ❄

17. Brave-Braver-Bravest

In good olden days there lived a prince. He was very proud of his bravery and skill. He was skillful in the art of archery. The shots of his arrow were very exact and to the point. His friends called him Arjuna.

Arjuna was married to a beautiful girl. His wife Prema wore a Nath or ring of gold in the left nostril. It added to her beauty because it was studded with glittering jewels.

Arjuna praised her nostril *Nath* or golden ring. It was big in size. An arrow could pass through it. To impress his art of archery on his wife he decided to shoot an arrow through the nose-ring. He asked his wife to stand still at a distance so that he could shoot an arrow through the nose-ring. She was shocked. If the shot misses it can be her end of life, or at least she would be a noseless lady. Who would like a woman with cut-off nose?

Prema did not want to annoy her husband. She obliged him and his arrow shot was exact. Arjuna felt proud and said, "What sort of archer I am?" Her modest reply was—"Before your art of archery I feel sigh".

Shooting the arrow through her nose-ring became his pet sport. His wife turned pale due to fear but she was helpless.

Once she visited her mother's house. Her girl-friends were surprised to see that her health was failing. They enquired whether her mother-in-law ill-treated her or her husband was misbehaving. She said, "All is well there. My husband is an archer. He shoots arrow through my nose-ring everyday. I am terrified when his arrow passes through my nose-ring".

One of her friends said, "Do you resent his action? She said, "After shooting his arrow he praises his bravery and I have to praise him".

One of her friends suggested her to say;

"Brave you are, but not the only brave,
People outside are braver, I bet.
Test your bravery among heroic men,
You may face even braver than bravest.

Prema returned to her in-laws house. Her husband repeated his old sport and asked to comment on his bravery. Prema said,

"Brave you are, but not the only brave,
People outside are braver, I bet.
Test your bravery among heroic men,
you may face even braver than bravest".

Arjuna never expected such a challenging answer from her. He jumped to the conclusion that some of her girl-friends must have instigated her to speak these words. They have poisoned her ears. He took her wife's words as a challenge. He decided to leave his home to search out braver and bravest man to challenge him.

In a deep jungle Arjuna saw a young man gazing at the sky. His eyes were not blinking. He said to him, "Why are you seeing in the sky"? He said, "Are you blind? See what a beautiful dancing scene in the sky. The most charming dancers in their decorated dress are showing best dancing postures. Do not disturb me".

When the dance was over he turned toward Arjuna and said, "What a poor sighted man you are. I am Nenu. My eyes are blessed with extraordinary power".

Arjuna felt ashamed to hear his bravery. He extended his hand of friendship to Nenu and related his life story. Nenu behaved proudly because he thought what was said,

"Brave you are, but not the only brave,
People outside are braver, I bet.
Test your bravery among heroic men,
You may face even braver than bravest."

Both of them marched on to search out a man braver than the bravest. As they moved to deeper jungles they noted a young-man drawing his arrow to shoot at a mark. They did not notice any sign of shooting mark. Arjuna said, "O young man, what are you shooting at? I see no mark of shooting".

Senu, the marksman said, "Three miles away from this place, a bee blind with right eye is sitting on a berry tree. I want to shoot its left eye". After a moment he jumped out of joy because he had hit his target successfully. He said, "I am the bravest man. I am matchless".

Nenu said, "I was also proudy like you. But now I say:

Brave you are, but not the only brave,
People outside are braver, I bet.
Test your bravery among heroic men,
You may face even braver than bravest.

Senu looked at them disdainfully. He accompanied them to find out braver than the bravest man. All of them marched on towards the deepest jungles. They saw a long and sturdy man standing in running posture. Senu said, "Why are you standing in such running posture? Have you gone mad?"

Lambu, the swift runner said, "From early childhood I am in habit of drinking doe's milk. A file of deer is just to pass through this place. I shall catch five does to milch them". The deer files came and he successfully ran after them and took milk to his satisfaction. Arjuna, Nenu and Senu were surprised to see Lambu's bravery.

When Lambu praised himself, Senu said,

"Brave you are but not the only brave,
People outside are braver, I bet.
Test your bravery among heroic men,
You may face even braver than bravest.

But Lambu's ears did not accept Senu's challenging words. All of them marched on to search out the braver than the bravest man.

They saw a dwarf resting under a tree. He was wearing a strange coloured cap in a shabby manner. All of them laughed at Kantopu and said, "why don't you wear this cap properly?".

Kantopu said, "If I wear this cap properly entire area will be frozen. Everybody will shiver with cold. Do not ask me to put it on orderly. I shall put on it orderly in the time of dire need".

All of them believed his words. They took him bravest among brave. They marched on to test Kantopu's bravery at proper time.

After crossing the jungles they reached a city. They came to know that the princess of that city had put a challenge to young-men. She claimed that she would marry a man who would defeat her in running race. But if the man is defeated he would be done to death by his father.

The friends looked toward Lambu and said, "This is the time to test your bravery. Accept the challenge if you are a true brave man. We shall help you if you so desire".

Lambu said, "I accept the challenge, I do not need your help. After all the princess cannot be married to all of us".

All the friends went to the king. He was sitting among his courtiers. Lambu bowed before the king and threw challenge to run a winning race against his daughter. His daughter was very proud, haughty and cunning also. She agreed to defeat the challenger like previous youngmen.

There was a pale water pond under a hill. It was about twenty miles away. According to the bet a man who brought a bucket full of pale water from the pond earlier would be the winner. He would be married to the princess. If he loses he would be beheaded.

Lambu, the fast runner, accepted the challenge. The princess and Lambu started running with buckets in their hands. Lambu reached the target on the spur of a moment. He filled the bucket from the pond's pale water and started running back. On his way back he thought that if he returned immediately the king might think him as a magician. He might go back from his words. The princess may be hardly half way of her onward journey. He took rest under a shady tree and felt fast asleep.

The princess noted it. She threw the water from his bucket and ran fast to win the race. Lambu's friends suspected something foul when he did not return. They talked among themselves. Arjuna warned them to be serious.

Arjuna asked Nenu to findout Lambu's whereabout. Nenu gazed with full concentration. He saw Lambu was sleeping under a tree. His bucket of water was spread over the earth. A cobra was coming down from the trunk of the tree to bite Lambu. The situation was most dangerous.

Arjuna asked Senu to find-out some immediate solution. Senu took out his bow and arrow. He shot the arrow on cobra's hood. The dead cobra fell on Lambu's chest with a thud. Lambu woke up. He immediately connected all the threads of the story. He remembered Nenu, Senu and their leader Arjuna.

He immediately picked up the bucket and again ran towards the pond. He met the princess on his way to pond. He showed no anger towards her. He filled his bucket again from the pond and reached earlier than the princess. He won the bet. He was a winner. People clapped for him. After some time the princess also returned with the bucket full of pale water.

Lambu won the race but the King refused to marry his daughter to him. He put all of them behind the bars. It was a chance for Kantopu to show his worth and bravery. He put on his strange coloured cap properly. The entire area began to freeze. The king and his daughter began to shiver due to untimely cold season. The royal astrologer told the King to free the young prisoners and to keep his words for marrying his daughter to the winner. The King realised his mistake. He freed the young-men and the environment became normal.

According to the bet the king offered his daughter to Lambu. Lambu refused to accept the offer. He said, "Credit goes to Senu. He shot dead the cobra which fell upon me and I woke up. Otherwise I had been doomed. Give princess to Senu. He is braver than me".

Senu refused to take credit. He said, "Nenu pointed out the situation to me. Credit goes to him. Give princess to Nenu. He is braver than me".

Nenu refused to accept the offer. He said, "Offer princess to Arjuna. He is braver than me. He can shoot an arrow through nose ring. He humbled down our false ego. He is a prince. He deserves the princess".

Arjuna refused to accept the offer. He said, "It is Kantopu, the dwarft, who saved our life and forced the King to marry his daughter to the winner. The real winner among us is Kantopu. He has proved that he is bravest among the braves".

The king was forced to marry his daughter to Kantopu, the dwarf. The princess realised that there are people braver than the bravest.

Arjuna returned home. He said to his wife Prema, "You were correct when you said these words to me.

Brave you are, but not the only brave,
People outside are braver, I bet.
Test your bravery among heroic men,
You may face even braver than bravest."

I faced braver, bravest and even braver than the bravest people in the society. It was my false ego which tortured you.

❄ ❄ ❄

18. The Crusader Badshah and Wise Wazir

Once there was a *Badshah*. He was a fanatic ruler. He was a crusader. He was known as Gazi. Not only he looted the public but also burnt their houses. Many children became orphans. Women became widows. The homeless people had to bear all the ill effects of bad weather. Old people were the worst sufferers. Generally epidemics broke out in the area after his attack. The villages gave a deserted look. People were fed up with his demon like cruel behaviour.

He shared the loots with his wazirs and relatives. They became rich, but off and on they also fell prey to epidemics. Once the only daughter of a wazir died of illness. It was a personal shocking experience for him. He was a wise person. He was forced to chalk out some plan to check the ill deeds and misadventures of his Badshah.

Once the Badshah was passing through a deserted village. He was accompanied by his wazir. A grave like silence prevailed in the area. At once a howling voice broke that silence. This howling was answered by a hooting on the other side. The Badshah wanted to know about those howling and hooting voices in the dead hours of night.

The wazir told him that the voice was produced by the owls. An other owl has answered his call. They want to tackle and settle their family problems. The Badshah showed keen interest in the owls. He said, "Do the owls have some family problems? They are birds. They have enough to eat. They face no challange to life as they flew only at night."

In the meanwhile there was a fluttering sound. An owl couple flew from their nest to a nearer tree and settled in a thick tree. The other owl couple welcomed the guests with a howling sound.

The Badshah said, "O wise wazir, you must be knowing the language of these owls. Will you tell me about their problem? I am the Badshah of a large state. I would like to help them."

The wazir said, "Let us move to that tree where this owl couple has settled. We can observe and listen to them in moon-lit night."

The Badshah and wazir moved stealthily to the assembling point of the owl family. They sat there silently. A whispering and slow hooting voice punctured by the rattling noise of leaves and branches could be heard by them. The Badshah asked his wazir to decode their conversation. The wise wazir hinted him to keep silence otherwise the owl families would be disturbed. He would tell their problem on return to their palace. The Badshah, though impatient, agreed to his suggestion.

When the Badshah and the wazir returned to the palace the armies were preparing to loot and destroy a nearby town as a part of their next crusade. Horses were neighing, Elephants were trumpeting, Swords and daggers were being sharpened guns and cannons were being tested. Gunpowder and other ammunition was being taken out from the magazine. The army columns were waiting for march order from the Badshah. They were to ruin not only the town but its every breathing inmate. The wazir had a glimpse of all the preparations and went inside the consultation room.

The Badshah was impatient to know the topic of owls' conversation. Seeing the Badshah eager the wazir said, "Badshah Salamat, the two owl families want to settle the marriage of their owlets-male and females. There was some serious dispute regarding offering of mehar, dowry and marriage party menu.

"Dowry and marriage party menu disputes even in owls' families"? exclaimed the Badshah. "What do they demand? Can I help them through my contribution? After all I am the ruler of this large area. I should take care for one and all."

The wazir revealed that the female side demanded two hundred deserted villages for their daughter as mehar but the male side can afford one hundred villages so far. There is an owl serving as middleman.

"Middleman in owls family!" The Badshah enquired. "What he is to say."?

The wazir told that the middleman was praying for Badashah's long life.

"O, even owls are praying to God for my long life," said Badshah surprisingly from his high seat."

The wazir said, "Yes, your majesty. The middle man owl was a assuring them that hundred more destroyed villages is a matter of a few months for our Gazi crusader Badshah. Let the preliminary formalities be settled. So far as the marriage menu is concerned for the party, all participants will enjoy their choicest food. The marriage night will be fixed when the kind Badshah attack the town as a part of his crusade. Old owls and vultures could pluck out the dead infants eyes. Young dead man's-women's liver and heart will suit youthful birds like crows, kites and hawks. Special invitees as jackals, wolves can pull out old man's intestines. "The marriage party may enjoy seven nights stay and relish sumptuous food...."

"Wise wazir, please stop, please stop. My ears can no more listen to this destructive description. The cries of orphans and widows are piercing my ears. I am a man not a Satan. You have opened my eyes. What Satanic acts I am doing in the name of crusade. I vow I shall never destroy any town. Ask the armies to stop the attack. The Badashah bowed his legs on the ground. He closed his ears with both the forefingers, and looked towards sky. It looked as if the crusader or Gazi-Badashah was repenting for his ill doings and praying god to forgive him. He never wanted to be sent to *Dojakh* or hell on the Dooms Day.

The wise wazir prayed with folded hands beside the Badashah. He saved the destruction of humanity in the name of religion.

❄ ❄ ❄

19. Can a Bullock Deliver a Colt

Once Ramdass the barber messenger had to deliver a *peeli chitthi* or auspicious marriage information letter to a far off village. He got up early in the morning to avoid the heat of the sun. He arranged proper fodder and water for his mare. He had developed a deep fellow feeling for his mare. When he conversed, with his mare it would respond by moving its tail, mouth or just by neighing. Ramdass understood this coded language.

He travelled a part of his journey by noon. Ramdass and his mare took full rest under the shade of a tree during mid noon. By sun set they reached near a village. Ramdass noted some unnatural behaviour of the mare. It might deliver a calf by night as it was in advance stage of pregnancy.

He knocked at the door of a big landlord and asked for shelter for a night. The landlord noticed the situation and allowed him to stay in his yard. His attendants arranged food and shelter for both of them.

By mid-night Ramdass noticed the movements of his mare. It delivered a beautiful young colt. The mare licked it to show its affection. After some struggle and pain the colt stood on its legs. Ramdass touched it time and again to show his love and affection. Both, mother and infant felt the emotional feelings.

Next morning the landlord came to know about the new delivery. He went to yard side. Ramdass thanked the land lord for his generosity and begged leave of him for his next journey.

As Ramdass moved with his mare and new born colt the Landlord said, "Where are you taking my colt? It is mine. One of my bullock delivers a colt every year. Where is my bullock? Have you stolen it.?"

Ramadass was taken aback. He reacted hesitatingly, "Zamindar Sohib, my lord, my mare has delivered it. Can a bullock give birth to a young one? Please do not cut joke with a poor traveller."

The landlord frowned and said," Do you not believe my words. Even village Panchayat will approve my statement. If you say I can call the meeting of village Panchayat."

Ramdass hesitatingly accepted Landlord's suggestion. He firmly believed that Panchayat can never deliver unjust judgement. It is a natural law that bullock cannot give birth to any calf. Moreover it is the mare which gives birth to either to filly or to a colt. Panchayat judgement would be surely in my favour. In no case it could be otherwise. More over I am a poor person. Panchayat is always very considerate.

The landlord sent his *karindas* or assistants to the members of the Panchayat. They were busy in convassing for the forthcoming elections. Faction ridden society in these days has complicated the selections, elections and even the judgements. Moreover powerful families and the money have tilted all equilibriums and balances. The candidates were surprised to hear about urgent meeting of the *Panchayat*. They did not even ask for the agenda.

The villagers also came to know about the meeting as also about the proposed agenda. They felt that there was no need for calling a Panchayat meeting for that purpose. Even a child can deliver this judgement. The colt belongs to Ramdass because his mare has given birth to it. How can a bullock deliver a calf. It is only cow which litters calves.

By evening people started gathering near the *Panchayat Chabutra* or platform. They were smoking the *huqqa* or a hubble bubble and gossiping. The members of the *Panchayat* were enjoying drinks of the land lord.

After refreshment one of the Panchayat member said," Raisahib, what is the agenda for discussion today?"

Other member objected sarcastically, "Not for discussion but for decision."

Not for decision but for our direction," said the third member."

"Tell in your calculated decision so that it can be publicly announced and accepted before the people. You are our benefactor and protector. You spend so much money on our elections. Not only members of your joint family are influential voters but your caste is deciding factor in all the elections, "said the fourth member humbly.

The landlord said, "Set aside all these oily words. Today I have faced a strange problem. A passerby sought shelter for night stay in my yard. He says that his mare has given birth to a colt at night. I say that my bullock delivers a colt every year. The colt is mine. I need the stamp of the *Panchayat* in my favour. The case is so simple."

The members saw each other's face. The benefits enjoyed by them as elected members danced before their eyes. The hardships which they can face if they do not favour the landlord also slid in their mind. They had developed taste for the power. Their eyes were lowered out of shame because the landlord showered money in their election. They were sharply divided between their inner and outer conscious. But inner conscious was well fed so it was bold.

Ramdass was sitting downstairs amid the villagers. They were consoling him to have courage. Sooner or later truth prevails. The members came down stairs along with the landlord.

Ramdass stood up with folded hands and asked for justice. It was announced that the colt belong to the landlord as his bullock gives birth to a colt every year. The bullock is missing. Ramdass might have untied its rope and it had strayed away in the jungle.

It was more than a bolt from the blue. The villagers murmured that judgement was most unnatural. The Panchayat decision was diluted by the money game. Justice became toy in the hands of caste, money and majority votes but Ramdass was still having a ray of hope. His inner self believed that he would be winner sooner or later. He saw some glitter in landlord's eyes.

Ramdass said, "Rai Sahib, I leave my mare here as a price for hospitality. The colt may die in its absence. As your bullock has strayed away this mare will feed it."

Rai Sahib said, "You feel disturbed take rest for a night. You will restore yourself."

Ramdass agreed. He served the mare and the colt throughout night?

Next morning Ramdass said "Rai Sahib, permit me to leave your house. Beside colt you can keep the mare also. I am on urgent mission this mare may help the Panchayat members at the time of canvassing the voters. It will be a good reminder to the voters of this incident. They will surely vote for them."

Rai Sahib read deeper meanings in Ramdas' sarcasting words. He said, "Ramdas you take your colt along with your mare. I wanted to test the role of money and power in elections. These are big spinners. Justice can dwindle in between the two. Poor may still cry for justice. The heat of his sighs may char the society like the bellows of blacksmith."

Ramdass was the winner. He petted his mare and colt. He marched on his destination. He was blowing hot and cold at that incident.

❄ ❄ ❄

20. Badlu versus Aayaa Raam-Gaya Raam

Badlu was a well known name in the area. He got this name 'Badlu' because his elder brother died as infant and he was born within one year of his death. His parents thought that God had blessed this son in return of their deceased one. Naming a child Badlu or Paplu in such cases is a common practice in the area. Both the names have the meaning-in place of or in return of. Badlu's peer group called him Nathu because his nose was pierced at the time of birth to save him from any untoward happening. But this was just his nick name.

As Badlu grew up he shared the work of his family. Once he had to go to his sisters-in-laws to offer some clothes on the occasion of some ceremony. He got up early because he had to catch a train. The station was about five miles away. He placed the *gathri* or bundle of the clothes on his head. He had good practice for carrying load on his head because he had to bring fodder from his fields daily.

Badlu reached railway station in time and bought a ticket. He enjoyed the song of a singer party which was very professional to attract travellers for selling *Beedi* etc.

When the train reached the station he took his seat in one corner of a compartment and placed his *gathri* or bundle of clothes by his side. Ticket-examiners were very regular in that train because checking tickets meant an extra income from the defaulters. One of the ticket-examiners was very cunning and funny. He used to cut jokes with the travellers just to pass his time happily.

The ticket-examiner noticed Badlu. He thought of cuting some joke with him. Badlu looked very innocent. This was his first journey by train. It was a novel experience. The ticket examiner asked him to show his travelling ticket. He untied the knote of his turban's corner and handed over the ticket to the ticket examiner most innocently. He examined it with keen interest. He turned and overturned the ticket time and again. He smiled. Badlu felt nervous.

The ticket examiner smiled and said," You are travelling on wrong ticket. Your long moustache show you are a man. But you are travelling on a female ticket. Badlu resented and said, "It is the fault of ticket seller. He might have not seen my long moustache."

But the T.T.I said," He may be under the impression that you are buying ticket for your wife. Did you ask to issue a male ticket."

Badlu kept mum. The T.T.I was happy because innocent Badlu was entrapped. Warning Badlu he said, "Be careful. Try to hide the ticket at the exit gate when you leave the station or you may be fined ten times." The T.T.I left the compartment. His fellow T.T.Is noted this scene amusingly. They said, "Why do you tease travellers just for nothing. You exploit their ignorance." The T.T.I said," I shall show most amusing drama to you without asking for any amusement ticket."

Train moved on station after station. Badlu felt disturbed when the T.T.I left the compartment. He thought a plan to save him. He went to the toilet along with his *gathri.* He put off his male clothes. He took out-female clothes meant as offer for his sister. He put on ghagra lengha or skirt-and *chunri* a tied and dyed female chadder. He hid his face with long veil. He put some bangles on his hands. He put on the *nath* or nose ring as his nose was already pierced,. To the best of his knowledge he looked like a woman. Now he felt him self safe as he had a 'female' travelling ticket as confirmed by the T.T.I.

The ticket examiner again visited Badlu's compartment with his fellow T.T.I.s. He recognised Badlu's bundle and a woman sitting by it with putting a long drawn veil on the face. This time they did not check his ticket otherwise he was well equipped with 'female' ticket. The T.T.I. just smiled as if he had not noted Badlu in his changed dress.

T.T.I said to his Colleagues T.T.Is, I shall show you a drama on the next station. You enjoy it without entertainment tickets. On the next station the T.T.I went to his co-worker who was standing on the exit-gate. He had some whispery conversation in his ear and came back.

Badlu set his bundle of clothes on his head very carefully. He checked that he covered his face well with his veil. He arranged the plates of his *lengha* properly as it was his first experience of putting on female dress. He set his bangles in his arm properly. He checked his nose-ring. He held the female' railway journey ticket in his hand with extra care.

When Badlu approached the exit gate in female dress the ticked examiner asked 'her' to show the journey ticket. Badlu showed the ticket to him without uttering a word from his mouth. The ticket examiner turned over the ticket time and again. He smiled. Badlu became suspicious but kept mum.

The ticket examiner said, "O, you have travelled on a 'male' journey ticket this is illegal. You will have to pay special fine for it. Put off your bundle of clothes from your head."

Badlu was shocked. It was too much for him. The previous ticket examiner declared his ticket as 'female' ticket. He cursed the railway system in his heart but he was still silent. Some other travellers passing by gathered there. The previous ticket-examiner team also came there to enjoy the scene.

Badlu was standing in between the two teams of ticket-examiners, One team saying the same ticket 'male' and other as 'female'. The traveller-fellow is same. Only he changed his dress under hard circumstances.

The ticket examiner turned toward Badlu and said, "*Bahenji,* you have to pay ten times money as fine, take out the money and clear the door. A mob has gathered here unwantedly give way to them. This is a government place."

This rebuke was too much for Badlu. He could not control his anger. He removed the veil from his mouth. He threw his *chunri.* He put off the nose-ring. Long moustache on his face attracted the attention of the mob. He threw his *lengha.* In all respect now he was male and he had a 'male' journey ticket. Why should he pay fine as punishment.

Badlu stood on a terrace and said, "This ticket has turned me as a political buffoon. Such person assume various political dresses in a day of this or that party for his own selfish ends. They are Aaya Raams and Gaya Raams. For heavens sake do not make railway ticket into a political party ticket. Ticket-examiners should remain ticket-examiners and not behave like agents of political parties."

The on lookers clapped. Badlu Ram said, "My name "Badlu' was given under certain circumstances. But I do not change colours like some political chameleons. My parents made hole in my nose as *Tona* or sorcery. I am not a nose cut off person. I am a respectful man."

Badlu and ticket-examiners, both discharged each other from offence and had their ways. Badlu related this incident to his friends when he returned from the journey. They still enjoy this episode and taunt their fellow politicians when they change their party.

❄ ❄ ❄

21. Gyani, Dhyani and Rambai

Once there was a priest. His name was Gyani. He earned his livelihood through preaching. He moved from place to place and related stories from holy books. His wife Rambai also accomanied him. She helped him in arranging and decorating the worship platform and other activities. The priest was simple but his wife was worldly-wise.

Once Gyani the priest, reached his village and settled there for a fortnight-preaching. Those were Kartic days. In the early morning the ladies had their bath in the village pond in starry nights. They worshiped *Pathwari Devi* the goddess of cross-roads. They lighted earthen lamps and offered morning prayers. The village was resounded by their prayers with songs sung in praise of Radha-Krishna. The priest's wife Rambai accepted their offerings.

At night the visiting priest, Gayani ji related stories from Kartic Mahatmy book. The village temple priest, Dhyani became jealous. Dhyani became Gayani's rival because his income was shared by the visiting priest. Dhyani incited some of his devotees to disturb his *Katha* or religious discourse by raising doubts, putting irrelevant questions and queries. Sometimes they let loose the village buffalo sire near the stage to disturbs the religious gathering. But his *Katha* was so interesting that the rival party could not succeed.

One day Gayaniji the visiting priest, was relating a story regarding Kamadev, the god of love and lust or the cupid. He said that only Lord Krishna could control lust. The danced with the Gopies or his female disciples and keep aloof from sexual lust. The power of lust is hundred times more than a powerful elephant. Keep women away or you may be allured by her attraction.

The village priest Dhyani raised a slogan against him. He said that the visiting priest is a *thug*. He is anti woman. He is misleading the society. He wants to create a dividing wall between men and women. He wind up his business. He raised slogans after slogans along with his followers. The religious assembly was disturbed. The devotees returned to their homes without offering Sidha or uncooked grain etc. to *Gayani* and the priest couple had to sleep empty stomach.

Next morning the visiting priest Gayani decided to move to some other village. His habit was to avoid shastrarth or doctrinal debate or discussion. At the end of his discourse he used to say to his listeners, "follow my discourse if you like or forget it," if you do not like." Discussion on matter of faith was sheer wastage of energy.

Gayani said to his wife Rambai, we shall move to next village. Dhyani, the local priest, did not like my yesterdays discourse. He said that I am raising a dividing wall between man and woman. He can control Kamadev or desire for lust. To night we slept empty stomach."

Rambai said," I am master of playing trick or feat. I shall be true to my name and do not feel disappointed. The shastra's saying is always true. It is time tested. Dhyani will admit his fault publicly. You will enjoy a public show."

Gayani gained confidence. He gave full freedom to his wife to arrange the show.

Rambai had developed very sympathetic contact with her neighbour. She went to the neighbour's wife and asked her to give her *payal manjir, nupur* or anklets with small bells for a night. She had some own ornaments which the devotees had donated to her.

After arranging the required adornment articles, dress, fineries and make-ups she disguised herself as young woman and went to Dhyani, the village temple priest. It was after sunset time. Dhyani had performed his Sandhya-Arti or evening worshipping. He had a dish burning with earthen lamps and incense.

Rumbai bowed before him and requested for night shelter under his protection as she was alone and forgotten her way. Dhyani ji, while muttering some *mantras* or sacred verses gave negative sigh by his hand and moved his back toward the woman. When she followed him he said "no"-"no"-"no" and entered into his hut.

Rambai said, "Please be bold and save my chastity from the robbers. They may snatch my ornaments and plunder my chastity. They may even kill me. Save my life, give me shelter this moon is witness between you and me.

Dhyani ji opened the door. He show her inside and bolted the door. Rambai bolted the door from inside. Dhyani ji sat on his *ashan* or seat and started telling the beads.

As night set in Rambai started her game. She moved her Payal. The bells from the anklet ornament resounded the silent zone of the temple. A cool breeze air gave it a rhythm. Dhyani ji dhyan or concentration was disturbed. It was a full moon night. Rajnigandhas meant for idol worship, were very fragrant. Rambai began to ring her anklet bells very rhythmically as if she was performing a dance as the flowers tossed Dhyani ji's heart began to throb. He became helpless. He knocked at the door and unbolted it from outside and asked the woman to open the door as he could not tolerate mid night cold.

Rambai refused to open the door. She said, "I have forgotten the keys and cannot search it out due to darkness. Please cover your self with your black blanket. I shall feel unsafe if you enter the hut at midnight. Lust is the most powerful force. I am a chaste woman."

When Rambai did not oblige Dhyaniji he climbed up the roof of the hut. He tore its corner. He removed one wooden beam and a squared rafter and tried to jump into the hut. He had a well-built body. In a hurry to jump he did not remove the full beam. So he was struck in between the beam and squared rafter. He tried again and again but all invain. His body was badly scratched. Few blood drops wetted the cottage floor, Rambai unbolted the door and came to his husband.

Like lust sleep is also a powerful force. It lulls a person to sleep even over thorns. So sleep over powered Dhyani ji and he had a nap many times. At last he became unconscious.

Dhyaniji used to blow his conch shell early in the morning. Most of the villager used to leave their beds after listening this pious sound. It was a bad omen for the village because no conch shell sound was heard by them.

When the devotees went for morning prayer they found the doors of the temple were not opened. They saw the door of Dhyaniji hut was open. It may be the act of some mischievous person. They could not believe their eyes when they saw Dhyani ji hanging in between the ceiling and beams. He was unconscious. Some young men broke extra part of the ceiling and pulled Dhyaniji down. The local Vaidyaji arranged best treatment and Dhyaniji came to his senses. No one dared to ask Dhyaniji about the incident.

Gayani ji arranged his evening discourse as usual. He noticed a man with some bandages on his body. He tried to recognize him. He noticed that, he was none else but Dhayaniji who had opposed him yesterday during the discourse.

To avoid any controversy Gayaniji changed the topic of his discourse. He avoided his reference towards the power of lust and Kamdev, the god of love. Gayaya ji jumped several pages of the text and started a new mythical story.

Dhayaniji stood up. He wanted to say something. Gayani thought that he is going to raise some other controversy. He hesitated. But Dhyaniji requested with folded hands to continue the same story in which he involved the power of lust and sex.

Gayani ji was surprised. Why this overnight change? He said, "Dhyaniji, yesterday you raised objection against the power of lust and sex. Why are you insisting to continue the same story? Let me speak on some other topic."

Dhayaniji said, "To night I have tested your statement from my own experience. I lost my patience when a lady visited my hut last night. Our mantras or surmises from our texts are time tested. Any doubt about them can invite unwanted troubles. I stand a testimony to them.

❄ ❄ ❄

22. Cunning Kirori

Once there was a merchant. His name was Kirori which means owner of crores of rupees. He dealt in wholesale rice business. He became very rich. He donated a part of his income on religious pursuits. He patronised wrestlers and athletes. Both these groups came to his rescue in hour of need.

Once some house breakers hatched a plan to commit a burglary in Kirori's *Haveli.* They searched the weaker portion in the back wall and marked it with colour for an easy identification at night. Kirori was very cunning. He spotted the mark and made a counter plan to foil their attempt.

Kirori went to a wrestler Kehri and explained the plan of the burglar. Kehri, the wrestler, assured him to kill the burglar. Kirori agreed to pay one hundred rupees as a reward.

After the deal was struck Kehri came to Kirori's *Haveli* at night well equipped with a strong staff fitted with iron rings at the ends. At night the house breaker made a hole at the marked spot and entered the merchant *Haveli.* Kehri wielded the staff with full force on the burglar's head. He died then and there. Kehri dragged the body and placed it in one corner of the haveli.

When the first burglar did not come out of haveli even after a long time his associates became suspicious. They thought that he may loot the whole money. The second associate also entered from the same hole and he also met with the same fate at the hand of Kehri. The third and the fourth associates were also done to death by Kehri. He felt proud because he was the successful winner in his deal.

The merchant was seeing all this stealthily. Kehri, having completed his assignment went to Kirori and asked him to pay four hundred rupees.

"Why four hundred? Our contract was for one hundred only," said Kirori.

"Because I have killed four burglars," Kehri replied.

Kirori reacted, "But you will be arrested by the police. I have an understanding with the police for killing one burglar only. They will arrest you because you have killed extra three men. If you want to save your life, better you leave my haveli immediately. I shall arrange for the disposal of these bodies my self."

Poor Kehri began to tremble. Four murders and fear of arrest by the police was too much for him. Kirori befooled Kehri and saved his money. He wrapped the bodies in white coffins and placed them in different corners. His next plan was to dispose off the bodies most cunningly without spending any money.

A sadhu of a math (an organisation of hermits) was well known to Kirori. He used to invite him for lunch on auspicious days. The Sadhu knew the art of casting out evil spirits and ghosts. He had a well built body. The villagers called him Sayana Sadhu an exorcist.

Kironi went to the Sadhu and said "O Sayana Sadhu ji, a ghost has entered my house in the mid night. He is wrapped in white dress. He hides himself in the corner of my *Haveli.* I shall offer you ample money as Dakshina if you help me in getting rid of that ghost. Please dispose him off to some other place so that he can never come to my *Haveli."*

The Sayana Sadhu consented to oblige his faithful devotee. He visited his *Haveli.* at midnight. Kirori showed him the ghost wrapped in white cloth in one corner. The Sayana Sadhu was fearless. He went near the ghost. He kicked it and loaded him on his shoulders. In the dead of night he disposed of the ghost far away in a jungle and had a sigh of relief.

The Sayana Sadhu came back with full satisfaction and informed Kirori. Kirori said, "Sayana Sadhu ji, your *mantra-yantra* or sorcery is failing you. Your magical formula did not work on that ghost. He has entered my *Haveli* again before your arrival. Please try once again."

Kirori showed the body of the second burglar which, he had wrapped in white cloth. Sadhu was surprised to see it again in the same corner. He did not lose heart. He put the body on his shoulder and threw the body in the river. It was still darkness. None noticed Sayana Sadhu.

Sayana Sadu was tired. He did not go to Kirori. He went to his *math* and had a sound sleep. He thought that Kirori will compensate him by donating a large sum of money. But Kirori was oily tongued as well as salty tongued. It all depended on the situation.

After sunset Kirori went to Sayana Sadhu because he had to dispose of two remaining bodies with much care. He offered night prayer at *math*. Sayana Sadhu smiled but Kirori pulled his face. Sadhu guessed at his face and said, "Does the ghost still haunts you. I disposed him off in a deep gushing river."

Kirori said, "You have to try your magic once again. He is still standing in a corner. Please visit my *Haveli* before midnight. The members of my family are badly frightened."

Sayana Sadhu scratched his matted hair time and again as if he was cursing the ghost. Kirori returned home. He had his dinner and waited for Sayana Sadhus arrival. Sayana Sadhu came silently. Kirori showed him the ghost in the corner. The Sadhu could not believe his eyes because he disposed it at twice with full care. But really it was a hard truth that the ghost wrapped in the same white cloth was lying in the corner.

He muttered some mantras seven times and picked up the ghost on his strong shoulders. This time Sayana Sadhu became furious as if he was ridden by the spirits of some ghosts. He had hidden an axe under his arm. It was not visible in his loose knee length cloak. He threw the ghost on a rock and cut it into pieces most mercilenly and had a sigh of relief.

Being satisfied to his inner core he returned to Kirori and showed the blood soaked axe to him as an evidence of cutting the ghost into pieces.

Kirori said, "Swami Syana Sadhuji better you leave this type of assignment for ever. Better you leave the *math* because your glory and majesty is failing. You have made three attempts to free my house from a ghost but it is still standing in the same corner."

It was too big a challenge for Sayana Sadhu. He jumped on the ghost and soon disappeared in the darkness of night. This time he thought of throwing it in a *jhera* or old well so that it may get struck in deep thick mud for ever.

As Sayana Sadhu threw the ghost with a thud a peasant working near the well in early hours was frightened. He ran towards the village. Sayana Sadhu thought that the same ghost was running back to Kirori's Haveli. He followed him. The man entered into Kironi's

Haveli. He was gasping. The man was none else but Kirori's *Karinda* or worker. Sayana Sadhu was badly exhausted by having carried two dead bodies. He reached Kirori's Haveli most desperately. Kirori requested him to take rest but he tried to enter forcefully to catch the ghost. Kirori never wanted that his *Karinda* may know about the Sayana Sadhus mission and the two should meet together.

Kirori said, "Sayana Sadhu ji, I was badly mistaken. It was not the ghost. It was our family *devta* or a revered person. He will not harm us. He is our protector and benefactor. He is very benevolent. I shall settle account with him peace fully at my own level. I am sorry I troubled you so many times. I shall invite you for dinner on some anfricious occasion in near future."

Sayana Sadhu left for his math. He was badly fatigued. He waited for a call from Kirori for some time. Kirori never obliged the Sadhu again. He saved his money and felt happy for his cunningness.

❄ ❄ ❄

23. The Green Parrot

Once there was a king. He had a beautiful queen. She had two children—a son and a daughter. He loved them very much. Once the queen fell ill. She was suffering from a incurable disease. While in death bed she used to observe a sparrow couple. Once the female sparrow laid two eggs it hatched them by providing heat from its breast. When two beautiful chicks came out from the eggs. It shares its food with them. The queen was impressed by the emotional touch of the bird's family. She would also embrace her children thinking that she may be departing from them very soon.

Incidentally the mother sparrow died. The male sparrow brought another female sparrow. It did not like those chicks. One day it threw them outside the nest and they died. The queen related this incident to the king. She asked her husband not to marry again if she died due to illness otherwise her children will get stepmotherly treatment at the hand of the next queen. The king gave her word and she died peacefully.

The ministers advised and insisted the king for a second marriage. The king agreed. The newly wed queen was enraged when she saw two younger children from his first wife. She started teasing the children. She gave them very little to eat. She rebuked them on pretty excuses. The king saw all this helplessly because second wife was generally not submissive.

One day, the newly wed queen asked the king to send away the children far away in the jungles so that they may never return home. The king ordered his assistants to take away the children to far away jungles to get rid of them. The assistants carried out the orders and took the children away, they were afraid and began to weep. Some passerby heard their cries. When the children revealed their parentage to him he brought them back to the royal palace.

They rejoined their family. But the queen again became furious and asked the king to get them killed in the jungles. When the king did not oblige her she went alone with the family to the jungle. She cut the boy into pieces and cooked his flesh. She served that cooked flesh to the king. The king was unaware of it. He thought that his son might have been killed by some wild animal. They came back to their palace.

The queen built a small hut for the girl in a royal garden. She felt very lonely. She became weaker and weaker. The queen thought that the girl will die soon.

One day a strange parrot perched on her window. It started singing a song:

My stepmother cut me to pieces,
My father relished the plate,
I became a green parrot,
For my sister's company sake.

When the girl heard the song she felt happy. She clapped and danced with that rhyme. The green parrot daily visited her hut and sang the same song. Now she could make out some meanings in that song. She never felt the absence of her brother, slowly she gained her health.

Once the step mother visited her hut. She was surprised to note that the girl was quite healthy. She was dancing and clapping. She noticed a green parrot sitting on the window of the hut. She tried to fly it away. It showed its obstinacy. It repeated the song again and again. She felt offended. She was irritated and became averse to it.

When she returned to her palace she talked about the green parrot before the king. The king did not believe his ears. He decided to see the green parrot him self.

Next day the king visited his daughter's hut. The green parrot was singing:

My stepmother cut me to pieces,
My father relished the plate,
I became a green parrot,
For my sister's company sake.

The king tried to understand the message conveyed by the parrot. The parrot was there to console and give company to his sister. The sister relished the joy of her brother's company. The king visited his daughter's hut daily to enjoy the parrot's song. The queen did not like it. She thought of getting rid of the green parrot.

One day the queen sit beside the hut. The parrot visited the hut as usual. It sat and sang the same song on the window. The queen had the same sharp edged axe by which she had beheaded the son and cut him in to pieces. She jumped upon the parrot abruptly and cut its neck. It was a great soothing surprise for the parrot.

By god's grace the green parrot turned into a boy again. The queen was surprised to see the step son standing before her. His sister recognised her brother. In the mean time the king also appeared on the scene. He was surprised to see his son and daughter standing side by side.

The son related the whole story to his father. The king could not tolerate the cruel behaviour of the queen. He banished the queen from his kingdom and lived a happy life with his children. He never thought of marrying again.

❄ ❄ ❄

24. Four Takas Advice

Once a farmer had to go to a nearby town for somedomestic purchase. He yoked his bullocks in his cart and started for the journey and on his way he came across a traveller. He requested the farmer for a lift. The farmer said, "I shall charge four *taka* or a copper coin as fare. If you can afford you are welcome. He searched his pocket and paid the fare. The farmer was happy.

The town was far away. The farmar said," Our destination is far away. Please tell some story or relate some proverbial saying to pass the time. The traveller said, "You pay money and listen. Why do you ask for free service?"

The farmer was surprised. He said," Do you charge for talking? The traveller said, "The value of talk amounts from one *taka* to one lac. Listen according to your capacity."

The carter said, "Tell me a talk amounting to one *taka*. Take money in advance."

The traveller said, "Listen a talk in exchange of one *taka*. If night falls on your journey take rest there. Before going to sleep announce—"I am sleeping here under the shelter of that animal who so ever lives at the place. He may please guard me."

The cartman said, "This is not a proverbial talk worth one *taka*. How can an animal protect any body?" The traveller said," God lives every where. That animal guards in name of God. Test my words in hour of need."

They had hardly covered some distance when the carter said, "Please tell me one more proverbial advice." The traveller said," Take out one more *taka* and listen." The cartman put one *taka* on his palm.

"Accept the judgment of *panch* or five persons. God speaks through *panchas,* "said the traveller.

The cartman said" I shall judge your proverbial advice in due course."

They travelled some more distance. The cartman became impatient. Offering one more taka to the traveller the carter requested to tell him one more proverbial saying.

The traveller said, "I am not doing any favour to you. I am telling you in exchange of money. Do not reveal your top secret even to your wife. A woman cannot keep a secret. She is helpless by nature.

The cartman welcomed the advice and kept it in his mind as a subject for test.

They covered most of their way during these talks. The cartman thought that asking these advice is very odd. Why not to ask one more. He is not spending anything from his pocket. He had paid him four *takas*. The cartman said, "Dear co-traveller, we are nearing our destination. Take one *taka* more and tell the fourth proverbial advice."

The traveller pocketed the fourth *taka* or copper coin, and said, "Never tell a lie before a king or in the court. One who speaks the truth gets heavenly satisfaction." The cartman thanked the traveller and they departed for their mission.

Days passed on. One day the cartman had to go out to some city. Night befell on his way. He was tired. He decided to take rest at night. He unyoked the bullocks from the cart, cleaned the place and spread his bedsheet. Before going to sleep he announced." Any animal who lives here may please listen to me. I want to spend my night here in his shelter and protection." After this announcement he slept fearlessly.

When he got up early in the morning he was surprised to see a dead snake near him. He concluded that some mon-goose lives there. It has killed the snake to protect him. God came to protect him in this form. The travellers saying was worth one lakh rupees and not just worth one *taka* or copper coin.

Time passed on. One day the same cartman was returning from his journey when he met five men. They were standing by the dead body of an old saint. Its body was covered with a tattered old quilt. One of them said, "This is an old saint's dead body. Place it in your cart. Dispose it off in a sacred river, you will come across. The will be his best last rite.

The cartman recollected the co-travellor's words who had said that God lives in the council of five men and they are to be obeyed. He placed the dead body in his cart and moved on. Soon he came across a river. He threw the saints old tattered quilt on the ground. He heard a jingling sound. He became curious. He was surprised to know that the quilt was packed with precious jewels and gold coins. He collected his new found wealth and placed it safely in his cart. He dipped the saints dead body in the river with due ceremony. On return he handed out the money to his wife.

His wife tried to know the source of getting that wealth. The cartman re-collected his old co-traveller's words that not to reveal your top secrets over to your wife because she will reveal it one day.

The cartman tried to avoid his wife's querry but on insisting he cooked a strange story. He said that on his way he was very thirsty. No water was available any where. Due to hot summer season flourished *aak* bushes or *swallow wort* were seen every where. I quenched my thirst by collecting milk or juice from its branches. As a result of this juice my eyesight was brightened. He visualised the feat of mother Laxmi, the goddess of wealth. He dugout the spot. To his great surprise he got this hidden wealth. Who so ever would take *aak-ka-doodh* or swallow-wort milk will get this sight.

The life style of carter's family was changed due to this easy acquired wealth. The neighbour' lady tried to know the secret source of wealth. On insistence the cartman's wife revealed the secret as told by her husband. The neighbour's wife tried to convince her husband to go and take *aak-ka-doodh* to acquire the miracle eye sight.

The neighbor told his wife that aak-ka-doodh is very poisonous. It turns the man blind. He can meet his death even. But the lady did not agree. Under this or that pretext she sent her husband in the jungle and gave him aak-juice to drink in sufficient quantity. The hen-pecked husband became blind. His wife became furious and took the case to the court.

The carter appeared before the court. He re-collected the old co-traveller's words that always speak plain truth before the king and the court to enjoy heavenly bliss.

The cartman revealed the truth before the court. The court said that the overbold manly behaviour of the neighbour's wife and hen-packed nature of her husband are responsible for his blindness. The cartman was sat free. He paid a *taka* for this advice but it worth lacs and also saved his life.

❄ ❄ ❄

25. Kurukshetra: The Ideal Battle Field

Lord Krishna tried his level best to resolve the dispute between the Kaurvas and the Pandavas. As a messenger he carried many resolution to settle the accounts amicably without shedding a drop of blood. But Duryodhan was a very ambitious and obstinate prince. His father, Dhritrastra had soft corner for him. When daggers are drawn the armies need some suitable place for war. It must have plenty of water, grass, shady trees and open ground for army camps. It must be inhabited by warlike people. They must be hardworkers. They should not have much attachment to their families. Work and nothing but work should be their guiding principle of life. Work not only for themselves but for the benefit of the society. They must have sound philosophy for art of living. If some one dies he should not be reported because human soul is immortal. It will take rebirth according to its deeds.

The area around Indraprastha was surrounded by kururashtra, kurujangal and kurukshetra. Mathura was also not very far off. Lord Krishna trodded these areas with a mission to select proper place for war.

One day Lord Krishna was crossing some fields near Kurukshetra. Farmers were tilling their fields. Members of their families, younger and old, were helping them. Some farmers were watering their fields and others were weeding out the unwanted plants. Herds of cows were grazing in untilled wasteland.

Lord Krishna felt thirsty. He saw a middle age man plaughing the field. To avoid heat of the sun he had covered his head with some coarse cloth. A pitcher of water was placed on a raised platform well covered by a cloth. Some implements like sickle scythe, long handled chopper, axe, and other flat bladed tools were scattered here and there.

When the peasant saw Krishna coming towards him he immediately guessed that the passerby was thirsty. He stopped plaughing and moved towards the water pitcher. Krishna was happy because the peasant was well prepared to serve water to him without asking. Krishna washed his hands and quenched his thirst. He felt the taste of the water. It was cold and not salty.

When the peasant was about to return to his work his wife came from village side. She had a big straw basket on her head. It was full of *jawaraa* or chopped green fodder meant for the bullocks. Due to heavy load she was walking a bit slowly. She was shiffing her neck to this or that side to lose the strain of the basket. She used her *dupatta* time and again to ward off the sweat. In one hand she was holding a metal vessel. It contained food for the peasant. Krishna was noting her mood. She was some what disturbed.

She tried to put off her load. Her husband helped her. She kept mum for some time. She did not open her month. Her husband, the ploughman, said, "You seem very uneasy. What is the matter. You always greeted me with smiling face to ease and relieve me from my fatigue." She kept mum and wept bitterly after some moments.

She told her husband that his elder son has been bitten by a cobra. He died due to snake bite. Neighbours are waiting for him to dispose off his body.

The middle aged peasant heard the news of his son's death due to snake bite. For sometime he remained composed. He broke his silence and said, "It is all God's wish. His death was predetermined by his deeds in impervious life. We should not shed tears for departed soul."

Krishna showed all sympathy to the peasant but he remained unmoved. Krishna was surprised to see such a detached person in that area.

The peasant said, "Our bullocks are hungry. They are at work since early morning. Let us feed them. I am also hungry. Dead person is gone. Let me take my meal. Let me finish the last part of my work. If peasants do not sow, the society will remain hungry. Work is worship. Our son will be borne again according to his deeds. Soul is immortal.

The peasant again started ploughing the field. He completed his job and returned home to perform early rites of his deceased son. Krishna observed every minute details. He also joined the last rite.

By night Krishna returned home. Pandvas were worried about him. Krishna told the Pandvas that he was in search of proper area for the war field and that he had selected the proper place. He related the whole story of the peasant to the Pandvas. They were surprised that such type of people live in that area.

The Pandvas recruited most of the youths in their army from that area. They were tough and will fight full vigour for the right cause. They gave their lives in Dharmashetra. After death they got their proper place in heaven. No one collected their human remains after cremation for consigning to the sacred river. It is believed that till date people do not collect human remains if their relatives die there because that is a sacred area. Youth from this area serve Bharat by serving in the Indian army. Indian army always fights for the noble cause.

❄ ❄ ❄

26. Disguised Chandaal

After winning the war of Mahabharat, Yudhishthir became the king of Hastinapur. He wanted to become Chakravrati Samrata, an emperor or king of kings. To claim one self as Chakravrati king, one has to perform a Ashvamedha or a horse-sacrifice yagna. It lasts for one year. The king sits as Yajamana (who pays for the performance of the sacrifice) in Yajna Mandap, a special pavilion for worship. It is surrounded by a sacred Patta or cloth to keep the place segregated and sacred.

When Yudhishthir sat on the Yajna-vedi or altar, Brahma wanted to test his worthiness for that honoured seat of justice. A Chakravrati Samrata sees one and all with the same eye-may be poor or rich, high or low, beautiful or ugly, fit or disabled. He does not discriminate between caste, creed, colour, regions or religion.

Brahma assigned this work to Dharma, the father of Yudhishthira. He also asked him to spoil the Yajna. Dharma felt happy and disguised himself as Chandaal, an outcaste or most despised of mixed castes. His skin was as black as a crow. His coarse hair were standing upwards on his head. He seemed to be a glutton. His cracked heels were bleeding. He was hefty and he looked very wretched.

It was well known that the king of Hastinapur was used to give food etc. He fed the beggars to their full in golden plates. So Dharma, guised as a beggar reached Hastinapur.

Bhima was the Dwarpaal or head guard of the Yajna Vedi. He said to Bhima, "I am hungry for the last four days. I am dying with hunger. Please let me go inside to have meals to my full. I have heard your king's name and fame."

Bhima said," My elder brother, the king, is busy inside in performing Yajna. He will not like to see you in this state. You look like a chandaal. Your entry will desecrate the Havana. I shall bring food for you, outside the tent."

The Chandaal became furious and said, "Do you know who is a Chandaal? A chandaal is one who is a blasphemer, who does not seek blessings of old parents, who tortures his wife, loves one wife and hates the second, who divorces his wife just for nothing, indulges in forbidden days like Purnima, Amavas Aikadsi, and does not marry his daughter at proper age. Such a person goes to hell."

Before Bhima could utter a word Dharma disguised as Chandaal said, "that woman is *Chandaal* who visit *tirtha* against the wishes of her husband, have affairs with a paramour, disrespect elders-in-laws, takes' meal before taking bath or before her husband and speaks ill of her partner among her friends".

Bhima tried to calm him down but Dharma went on further explaining the characters of a *Chandaal.* He said, "*Chandaal* who disallows cow from drinking water, pushes it away though grazing in others' fields, charges fee for cow grazing spits in water, and puts off fire with foot. Have you noticed these characters in me."

Bhim was stunned to hear such sermons from a vulgar looking person. The disguised Dharma continued," A Chandaal is one who shows cowardness in war when confronting a powerful enemy, who does not fulfil his words, who is deceitful, considers virtue as vice, and who is a parasite. What right have you to call me *chandaal?*"

The disguised Dharma, though with cracked bleeding heels, was standing on firm footing. He said, "A *chandaal* is one who mixes honey with curd or mix sours in *kheer* enjoyments, eats without brushing teeth, who speaks ill of his teachers or indulges in unwarranted discussions with saints on undisputed topics, and perform *yajna* without chanting *mantras* or sacred verse."

"Listen to me *dwarpall*, donkey is *chandaal* among animals, a Kikar or Acacia is *chandaal* among trees. Do not seek shelter in its shade. Crow is *chandaal* among birds.

When words of learning were flowing from the tongue of an ugly looking man, Bhima could not keep praising his black-beauty. He said," I have all praise for your looks. Our door feels hunoured by your presence. You are so virtuous that we have all praise for your knowledge. I request you with folded hands to take your seat for a while. We will fulfill your wish. I shall convey your message to the king."

Bhima approached Yudhishthira and said," A holy man is waiting at our door. Though his looks are as ugly as that of a Chandaal yet impressed me by his valuable knowledge. Please invite him yourself. Do not raise any doubt about him. If he goes away hungry our Yajna will bear no fruit."

Yudhishthir was in a suspense to meet a chandaal like visitor. He said, "Oblige him by giving what so ever he wants. We are chanting Vedic hymns for Yajna. Why to allow him here? His presence here is most unwanted. The priests present here will feel highly offended by his looks. Even his shadow will offend these seers and they will not take their meals and so they will remain hungry."

As Bhima was already impressed by the visitor's knowledge he pleaded that we should not go by his *chandaal*-like looks. Nectar-like immortal words flow from his tongue. Let us be sure that he is a *saarang* or incarnation of Shiva. A great soul resides in his body. He is some *Devata* or revered person. It you do not attend him and he returns hungry, our Yajna will remain fruitless."

Unfortunately Bhima returned without any commitment and said to the beggar, you kindly tell me your inner desire for coming here please speak plain truth. Please tell, why are you so much tormented?"

The visiting guest remained well composed and said, "Why should I tell you? A king directly converses with a king. A minister exchanges views with his counterpart privately. A yogi or an ascetic is worthless without knowledge. A woman is worthless without husband. A city loses its glamour without a footman why should I reveal myself without my befitting counterpart?" I want to maintain my status."

Bhima accompanied the guest to the inner gate. A curtain was raised between the king Yudhister and the guest to maintain the sanctity of the *Yajana.*

The guest praised the king and said that a Raja is the rearing and protecting force of his subjects. He is father for the orphans. He helps the poor. He arranges marriage of orphan and poor family girls. I am your guest. You fulfill my desires. In return you will get its reward hundred time more than Yajnas. You should mix with me as two waters become one after meeting each other.

Hearing these words *Yudhishthir* pulled down the curtain and bowed to his feet. He said, "your presence has enhanced our honour. We feel honoured by welcoming you. You are either some *Devata* or *Brahma, Vishnu* or *Mahesh.* You may be *Indra* or our father Dharma himself."

The guest was not swayed by Yudhishthir praise. He said, "A Devata is sweat spoken, loves poors, serves others in needy days, never runs away from war and keeps honour of his family. He controls his mind and passion. He also visits religious places and arranges religions discourses."

Hearing these words from his tongue Yudhisthir praised his inner beauty of soul. He praised his knowledge. He praised his own fortune and invited him inside to take meal honourably.

The guest refused to oblige him. He said, "Taking donation from king is very sinful act. A king collects funds by taking people mercilessly. He charges money by penalsing cruel people. He taxes slaughter houses. He even charges taxes from brothel houses. This money is soaked with sins. If I accept your food or donation I shall lose my *Dharma, Karma.*"

Yudhishthir was surprised by his logical speech but he responded, "One becomes kings after long *tapasya* or ascetic fervour. He is like a lotus flower. He keeps the kingdom in stable state. If there is no king robbers will have their days and ways. If he collects taxes he spends them for religious causes also."

The guest still argued and said, "A king lives very busurious life on public funds. He inflicts enormous sufferings on his subjects. He gives death sentence to people. I will not take your meal. It is impious. I shall take my food from an orphan or I shall live just on fruit and roots of different sorts. If I accept your meal I shall go to hell."

The priests who were sitting around *havan-kundas* or fire pits heard this conversation. They became rebellious why should they accept food and *dakshina* or money from a king which is so impious? If they accept it they will go to hell. They left their seats. King Yudhishthra was highly disturbed under these circumstances. He requested the priests and the guests to stay calm and pray. Highly impressed by the courteous behaviour of Yudhishthira the "guest" was fully satisfied that he is just and religious king. He is not swaged by caste, colour or creed. He admits his ignorance and fault. He has proved himself a real king from all angles. He deserves pardon.

Dharma, Yudhishthar's father came to his real form and said," I am proud of my son. I have all praise for your mother, Kunti, who gave birth to such a son. Devatas will ever praise you in the time to come."

Dharma, the visiting guest, requested all the priests not to go to forests but to complete the Yajna. He also requested them to join community meal with the king.

❄ ❄ ❄

27. Sita Samadhi

In good olden days the bride chose her suitor through *Swayamvar.* According to this tradition the would be bridegroom had to show his worth publicly by performing the desired fete. Ram Chandra, the prince of Ayodhya, won Sita, the daughter of King Janaka, in a *Swayamvar* ceremony by uplifting and breaking Lord Shiva's *Dhanush* or bow. No one else but Ram Chandra was able to show this outstanding fete from the assembled suitors. Sita garlanded Ram Chandra and they got married.

Later on Ram Chandra had to go for an exile for fourteen years according to the wish of his father, Dashratha and step mother Kaikeyi. Ravana the king of Lanka stole Sita from her cottage when Ram Chandara was away for hunting a deer. Nala and Neel helped in construction a bridge over the sea. Even a squirrel helped Rama by wrapping sand on its wet body Rama blessed it by touching his fingers. It is believed that Ram conquered Ravana and brought Sita back to Ayodhya after exile was over.

Once a washerman's wife remained away from him for a night. When she returned next day he did not accept her. He said, "I am not Ram Chandra who accepted Sita though she remained in Lanka with Ravana for many months."

When a spy brought this incidence to his notice Rama was shocked. He never liked that even an ordinary citizen may raise a voice of dissent against him.

When Ram Chandra was thinking about Sita's abandonment he heard a murmuring complaints from his own house. It was none but his sister Shanta. She told Rama that Sita loved Ravana. She remembers him in many ways.

Ram was surprised to hear those words from his sister's mouth. He asked her to give some evidence for her belief.

Shanta told that yesterday Sita was cleaning utensils by putting dry hearth ash on a wet metal plate. She drew Ravana's sketch on the plate by her forefinger. When she asked her about the sketch she told that it was Ravana, Lanka's king. When she further asked her to mark some specific sign to show that it was Ravana, she marked a mole on Ravans thigh. Thigh is a hidden part of body. She had scanned his fleshy and hidden thigh with a mole as drawn by her on the plate. Though backbiting by brother's sister against her sister-in-law is a common human behaviour but washerman's remarks against Sita added new colour to the incident. Rama decided to renounce Sita and banish her. Sita cursed her sister-in-law to become a Taitihari or a stand piper. She would lay its eggs on the ground and people and animals would trample them.

Sita gave birth to a son who was named Lava. One day Sita went to fetch water from the river. Rishi Balmiki who looked after them found the cradle without Lava. The *Rishi* thought that some stray animal had taken away the baby, he placed *Kusha*, a sacred sharp ended grass, in the cradle. The *Kusha* was turned into a baby by *Rishi's* influence. When Sita returned with Lava in her lap she was surprised to see a baby playing in the cradle. Balmiki told her about his fear. The baby was named *Kusha*, after the name of that grass.

When Lava and Kusha grew up they wanted to know about the cause of her banishment and that too during pregnancy period. Sita told them a story of her childhood.

While in Janakpur a parrot couple was sitting on the branch of a tree in her garden. She caught the female companion and put it in a cage. She was delighted but the couple screamed. She paid no heed to them. The female parrot was pregnant. It was feeling the separation of its male companion. When it saw Sita laughing instead of showing mercy it cursed her. It said that she too would be separated from her husband during pregnancy days. She suffered this banishment during pregnancy period due to that curse. God is righteous. He never faulters his judgment. She got retribution of her unkind act. Lava and Kusha got answer of their curiosity.

Lava and Kusha used to graze their cows in *Ashrama's* pastures. One day they were tending their cows when they saw two matted hair men. They bowed before them with full reverence. These guests were Rama and his younger brother Lakshman. Rama enquired about the parents of those beautiful children. They said that the name of their mother is Sita. They expressed their ignorance as regard their father. Rama was surprised to hear their answer.

Rama said, "We are thirsty. Will you take us to the cottage where your mother lives."

The boys agreed. They moved from one forest to another. Fortunately when they were moving towards Sita cottage, Sky was overcast with dense clouds. It was due to Sita's magnanimity in that region. Soon all ponds and well were filled due to torrential rain.

As they neared the cottage Rama saw that due to sense of decency and shyness their mother Sita was drying her hair taking a cover under the tree. They asked their mother to cover her head as two persons by the name of Rama and Lakshman were standing outside.

Sita could not believe her ears. Out of deep anger and anguish Sita said, "You are telling a lie. You belong to the family of liars. He banished me. Why should he now come to me. I would not like to see his face."

But when Sita looked towards his son she notice that Rama, her husband, was standing before her. She could not believe her eyes.

She felt sorry for the words she used for Rama. She requested mother earth to take her in its lap.

It is said that earth caved in and Sita began to sink into the earth due to extreme shame, sorrow and sufferings. Moreover she was *Dhartiputri*, or daughter of earth. She came out of earth when Raja Janak was ploughing a field as ordained by a religious priest. Rama ordered Lakshman to pull Sita out of the hole. Lakshman ran swiftly towards Sita. He could hold her hairs. He tried to pull her out with full force. Her hair were turned into Kusha, the sharp edged grass. Both his palms were split with sharp grass. It is believed that the lines on our palms are marks of that unforgettable happening.

While Sita was sinking in earth a resounding voice announced, "O Rama, the ground where I am sinking, will ever remain fresh with green grass for your cows. Your present and coming generation will milk those cows and remain healthy. This land will remain *Annapurna* for your progenies, to feed them for future.

❄ ❄ ❄

28. Lakshmi and Tota

Lakshmi, the Goddess of wealth lived a happy and prosperous life. Her abode was on a *peepal* tree. Sometime she moved to a banana tree. Both are considered favourite abodes of Lakshmi. Many stories are connected with these abodes and her liking for them.

Lakshmi was proud that so many people name their children after her name. Dhanwanti, Dhanpati, Lakshmi, Lichhmi are very common names for the girls. Lakhimal, Kirorimal, Dhanna are very popular names for boys.

She was happy because she was churned out with fourteen *ratnas* or the fourteen precious treasures churned out from the ocean at the time of sagar manthan. She chose Narain as her husband and added her name as prefix to him. So he is known as Lakshmi Narain.

She was happy because she is well protected and guarded in safest places. She is worshipped in the temples and Diwali festival is specially dedicated to her.

Lakshmi shunned tota pennary the symbol of poverty, want, scarcity, hunger, unhappiness, misery and so on.

Tota lived in a thorny *babool* tree found in desert area. He is generally thirsty due to lack of rain and water. He likes draught, fighting, squiblings, misfortunes, vices, disputes, slander, villainy, wickedness, ignorance and so on and so far. He too is proud of his character. He feels that a poor person can have a sound sleep. He in not afraid of theft. A poor man always remembers God while rich man forgets him. Even Kunti, Pandwas' mother, wanted sufferings so that she could always remember Lord Krishna.

One day Lakshmi was resting under a shady *Peepal* tree at midday. Tota was going to desert side. He noticed Lakshmi and went to her. Lakshmi paid no respect to him. Tota said, "Lakshmi, you are very proud. Bidding good morning or good noon is a minimum courtesy. I am elder than you. All cow a bow before me from a reasonable distance."

Lakshmi reacted and said, "People respect me more. They always keep their doors open to welcome me. They hate you. They bid goodbye to you from distance. They keep their door shut for you. They pray to God that Tota should never come to their house."

Tota said, "You are the cause of so many ills and bad practices. All lootings, theft, bribery, paid killings are due to you. You are the cause of so many diseases. A rich man spends a sleepless night and...."

Lakshmi interrupted his abusive speech and said, "Why do people resort to looting and arson, because they are poor. You are the root cause of numberless sins."

It looked as if there was no end to their charges and counter charges. Their discussion took a heated turn. Incidentally a passerby saw them. He tried to pacify them. He wanted to know about them and the cause of their wrangling.

Lakshmi said, "I am Lakshmi, the Goddess of wealth."

Tota said, "I am Tota,"

"Tota" said the passerby, "You need not give me your introduction. I know all about your doings."

Tota was happy that he is a well known personality. His name and fame is every where.

"But what is the cause of your heated exchange?"

Lakshmi said, "I am more powerful. I am very charming."

Tota said, "I am more powerful and charming. You decide our case. You become our judge. We accept you as mediator. Otherwise I will not let you go. I shall follow you through out your life.

The passer-by found himself in a very unenviable position. If he says Tota is powerful Lakshmi will be annoyed and feel offended. She may leave him for ever. He will become a poor man. If he announces the case against Tota he will never forgive him. His life will become hellish.

The passerby took his seat on the *peepal* tree platform. He scratched his head. He kept mum for some time and thought of a funny plan.

Tota said, "Please give your judgement immediately. Do not delay. I have to visit many houses. I will visit your house also. I can make your house my permanent abode."

Lakshmi said, "Mr. Tota, you are threatening the judge. It is against law." "Give me a chance to think and reason. Give me time to find some reasonable solution. My judgement will have a far reaching consequence," said passerby

The passerby gained some confidence. Lakshmi's words consoled him. He said, "I have heard your talking styles. I will now judge your walking style also. Who so ever shows better walking style will be the winner.

Lakshmi and Tota agreed to his suggestion. The destination was set at a distance of about 500 yards away, up to a babool tree, which was Tota's residing place. They were to cover this distance with a swift speed. Both of them were to cover this distance one by one in order to get a right and unfaultered judgement. Tota opted for first chance because it was towards his residence. He left for the destination with a warning to the judge that he would not go away with Lakshmi during this period.

Tota moved swiftly with gaiety towards his residence. The judge was highly impressed by his walk. While returning he was but slow. He might he thinking about his sure victory. The judge commended his onward charming style of walking.

Now it was a chance for Lakshmi to prove her skillful walking. She was walking very slowly because that was Tota's residence. Tota was laughing on her way of walking. On way back she came with gaiety because she was returning to her place of residence. The judge commended her way of down walking. Tota was also keenly observing her walking style.

Both Lakshmi and Tota requested the judge to deliver his seasoned judgement because both of them had proved their worth.

Fortunately the judge was very shrewed and cunning. He did not want to displease either of them. It was in his intention that both of them should win.

The judge said, "Tota's walking style was praiseworthy when he was going away. Lakshmi's walking style was very fascinating when she was coming back to us."

Both Lakshmi and Tota felt happy over the judgement and they had their way. People still feel happy when Tota or poverty goes away and also when Lakshmi, goddess of wealth comes to them.

❄ ❄ ❄

29. Mahadeva-Parvati and Ganga Snan

Mahadeva or Lord Shiva lives in his own *Loka*. It is known as *Shiva-Loka*. Parvati also lives with him. They always wander from place to place. It is believed that the devotees of Shiva get a place in *Shiva-Loka* after their death by his grace.

Once Parvati desired to visit *Mrityu-loka,* the planet earth. She wanted to know how people on the earth spend their lives. Mahadeva told her that people on earth are in great trouble due to their own doings. Our *Loka* is far better than *Mrityuloka*. Parvati insisted time and again to see those people from her own eyes and satisfy her curiosity.

Mahadeva agreed to oblige her. They rode on their *Nadiya*, Shiva's bull, and reached planet earth in the twinkling of an eye. For some days they lived at mount Kailash. Parvati came to know that the river Ganges came down from heaven on this place known as Bindu Sagar and flew downward to Hardwar and Garh Ganga regions. People throng in lakhs to take bath in the ganges to wash off their sins. There is a big mela or fair on its downward ghats. Parvati desired to join the mela.

Mahadeva said to Parvati, "People may recognise us. They may throng us to touch their feet. They love and worship us in many forms-idols and otherwise. It will be difficult for us break their siege."

To avoid any untoward incident they decided to disguise themselves as husband and wife by putting on rural dress. Mahadeva became a simple peasant and parvati wore *lahanga-chunri*. When they were moving from place to place Parvati was surprised to see uncontrolled mob moving towards the *ghats* or river embankments. Parvati was highly pleased to note that people are to much religious.

But a question troubled her mind as Mahadeva had told her that those who sincerely take bath in the Ganges go to heaven. Mahadeva gives them space in his own *Loka*. If all these people will come to Shiva Loka it would be overcrowded. They will create many problems for Shiva Loka.

Parvati put her query before Mahadeva. Mahadeva laughed on her innocence. Mahadeva told her that there are very few people who had come for *Ganga-snana* with full religious mind. Some are here to avoid their heavy home responsibility and works. Some have come just as a pastime. Others are here to show how religious they are. Some people will relish foods of their choice. Some have come to meet their relatives who will also visit this fair. Some are here to earn money out of the sale of their articles. There may be some pickpocketer, thieves, or pilferers. Among this crowd many are beggars. There are elderly men and women who have come after marrying their daughters. They are here just for thanks giving ceremony to mother Ganges. Rare among rarest people are here to take real *Ganga-snana*. He will give them space in his *Loka*.

Parvati was annoyed to hear such a sad commentary about that crowd. She sharply reacted that she would not accept his comments in toto. She would like to judge his remarks. Mahadeva said, "Man's behaviour is not only duplicate but very complicated." He had a hearty laugh. He accepted her challenge.

Mahadeva suggested Parvati to disguise herself as a beautiful woman. He would become a leper. He suggested that she may ask the passer-by to dip me in the Ganges. The Ganga water will cure Leprosy. Only some sincerely religious man will come to help us. He will get *Shivaloka*. Parvati agreed.

Disguised Mahadeva-Parvati sat near a *Ghat* on a thorough fare. Many people passed by that way and noticed them with sorrow or sympathy. Some cursed the woman's parents because they gave their daughter in marriage to a leper. Some cursed the fate of the woman. Some praised leper's fortune to have such a beautiful wife. Some passers by turned their face to avoid the ugly look of the leper.

Some dandy youngsters passed indecent remarks on Parvati. Parvati became shy and restless. It was too much for her. Mahadeva smiled in the core of his heart because Parvati was suffering for her having doubts on Mahadeva's words.

Some *Sadhubabas* saw Parvati with desiring and longing looks. Even some suggested her to desert the leper and accompany them. It was too much for Parvati. She was badly shaken. She never expected that she would face such a humiliation in the presence of her husband.

Many passerby came. Parvati requested one and all to lend a helping hand in giving a bath to her husband in mother Ganga. A bath in the Ganges will allay his leprosy. If his leprosy disappears she could live a happy family life with him. But none came forward. All neglected her appeal. They rather scorned her. Touching the pus of a leper means inviting hellish sufferings.

Parvati was disappointed and felt dejected with human behaviour. Mahadeva consoled her by saying that sympathetic people still exist on this earth. No society can live without them though they are few and far-between, said that she cannot see him as a leper for such a long time. She showed her willingness to go back to their own *Loka* and never to return again on earth. Mahadeva convinced her to have patience.

At last a thin and lean man gazed the couple with sympathetic look. He himself requested them for some help. Parvati felt pity on him. How can he lift Mahadeva's heavy body up to the Ganga water?

But Parvati repeated the same words for a helping hand as she had requested so many passerby. She also warned him to be more careful in lifting her husband because this terrible disease can contact him.

The passerby said, "If your husband is cured by touching *Ganga jal* at my cost I shall be most happy because you will be able to spend a long-long happy life with him. One should learn to live for others also and especially for the disabled.

As this man extended his helping hand towards the leper Shiva came to his real body. The passerby recognised him. He was none else but Lord Mahadeva himself. The lady turned into Parvati. The man bowed before them most respectfully. He thanked his stars to see Mahadeva-Parvati on earth with his own-eyes. Mahadeva-Parvati looked each others. They blessed the passerby for being kind towards distressed and disabled. Soon after they disappeared from the scene.

❄ ❄ ❄

30. Bhartrihari

Once Bhartrihari ruled Ujjain, a most religious city. He was very beautiful and charming. One day he was taking his bath in the courtyard of his palace. A hot water drop fell on his back. He thought that some bird has dropped it. When he saw upward he noted that his mother was standing in the balcony. She was wiping her tears. Bhartrihari realised that the hot drop was nothing but his mother's tear. But why mother's tear? It was a mystery for him.

After taking his bath he went to his mother and said, "O dear mother, why a tear dropped from your eye when I was taking my bath? She tried to avoid his question but when her son insisted time and again she said, "your father's body was as charming as yours. It had a golden luster. It has gone to dust. So I wept. Your body too will go to dust one day. Why do not you renounce the worldly pleasures and devote yourself in God's devotion. The worldly pleasures are delusive. If you become a Bhakta, you will become immortal."

Bhartrihari had great devotion for his wife Pingla. Why should he renounce a wife who loves him so much? He paid no heed to his mother's words.

One day a Sadhu came to his palace. He had a strange golden fruit in his hand. Giving the fruit to Bhartrihari he said, "O Righteous king Bhartrihari, you take this *Amarphal*. One who eats it becomes immortal. Bhartrihari thanks Sadhu for his generosity.

As the best loving thing in the world to Bhartrihari was his beautiful wife Pingla, he wanted to oblige her. He offered that *Amarpahal* to her to make her immortal.

Wise men say a beautiful wife is enemy to her husband. Beauty is generally flint. It is gazed and praised by hundred others for their own selfish ends. So was Pingla

Pingla was in deep love with a royal horse-keeper. She wanted to oblige her paramour. She went to him in odd hours. She offered it to him with the request to take that *Amarphal* to become immortal. She wanted to enjoy his youthful years for a long period. The royal horse-keeper was overjoyed to see *Amarphal* and its influence on life. He stored it in a safe place.

Next morning he had a second thought. He loved and liked the royal dancing girl. He used to go there to enjoy her dancing skills.

He used to offer her lot of money. She served him with a variety of wine and drinks. He decided to present that *Amarphal* to her.

Next night the royal horse-keeper visited the brothel. When the dancing session was over by late night he opened a bundle. It contained a glittering object. The royal dancing girl was amazed to see that golden object. She snatched it from the horse-keeper. The horse keeper said, "My dear love, this is not gold. This is *Amarphal*. One who eats it becomes immortal. I wish that your beauty may remain forever, I have brought it for you. You take it in my presence for my satisfaction."

The royal dancing girl said, "Such chaste things are taken only in the morning after taking proper bath. I will pray to my Gods before eating it." The royal horse-keeper praised her gesture and left with full satisfaction.

The royal dancing girl thought that her life was very useless. Why to be immortal in such an immoral life. Enjoying worldly pleasures for a long time is a curse. Why not to offer such a valuable present to some dignified person. His life will be more useful for the society. She postponed her decision for the next day.

At night Bhartrihari and Pingla exchanged love stories with each other. Bhartrihari told her a strange story of extreme love for each other. He said that once a hunter went out for hunting. He hunted a deer. Its arrow was so sharp and to the point that the deer died then and there. Its doe could not tolerate its separation. It also died on the spot. Fortunately or unfortunately a cobra bit the hunter. He became blind and died. When the news of hunter's death reached his wife she could not bear the news of her husband's death. She gave up her life. Wheat a true love for each other. The night of young couple was over in relating this or that love story from both sides.

When the royal dancing girl applied her mind to search out a proper deserving man for taking the *Amarphal* it was Raja Bhartrihari. She loved Bhartrihari very much and he too loved her. She used to join dancing session in the royal palace. She decided to handover *Amarphal* to Bhartrihari, the beautiful and righteous king.

Next day she went to the royal palace. She met Bhartrihari with all due respect and regards. Bhartrihari received her properly. When Bhartrihari asked her the purpose of her visit in day time she said, "I want to offer you a matchless offer. It will immortalize you. The public will always remain happy under your judicious rule. I offer you this Amarphal. Please eat it and become immortal."

She offered the *Amarphal* to Bhartrihari. He observed it carefully. It was the same present which a Sadhu had presented him. He was stunned to receive it back through a royal dancing girl. He asked her about the man who had delivered it to her. After a lot of hesitation and reservation she revealed that the royal horse-keeper, his lover, had offered it to her he wanted her to become immortal but she did not like her present life and profession. You deserve it most because I like and love you for various reasons.

When the royal dancing girl left, Bhartrihari's palace he called Pingla, his beloved queen. Bhartrihari's said, "O dear Pingla, have you eaten the *Amarphal* which I gave to you?" Pingla replied in affirmative.

Bhartrihari observed her facial expression and said, "Take one more *Amarphal* to become double immortal". Saying these words he threw that apple in her lap. She noted that it was the same *Amarphal* which she offered to her paramour, the royal horse-keeper. She turned pale.

Bhartrihari asked his courtiers to present that royal horse-keeper before him immediately to judge the royal dancing girl's statement. The royal horse-keeper was presented before Bhartrihari. He revealed unreservedly that queen Pingla offered it to him and he passed it on to the royal dancing girl whom he loved so dearly. Everything was crystal clear before Bhartrihari without a grain of doubt. The infidelity of his wife Pingla, was exposed from all corners. Bhartrihari himself was a part of vicious circle. He cursed and reproached himself also. He recollected his mother's hint in which she had asked him to renounce the worldly pleasures.

Bhartrihari decided to become a *Sadhu*. In those days *Gorakha Nath* was a great Guru. He was a *Siddha* or a semi divine being of great perfection. He was a *Kanphata Sadhu* with slit-eared. He preached his teachings among common folk by walking from one place to another with his *Jamayat* or assembly.

Bhartrihari approached his *peeth* or *Dhooni*, a place where a sacred smoke-fire burns around the clock. He requested Gorakh Nath to accept him as a disciple by putting *Mudras* or long ear rings in the middle of his ears. As a first reaction he refused to accept his request because his wife will be a sufferer. When he related the flirt behaviour of his wife Gorakh Nath said in the heart of his heart that Bhartrihari will definitely miss her sooner or later. There is one way out.

Gorakh Nath said, "You wear the dress of *Nathpathy*. Wear string of beads around your neck and arms. Always bear *chimta*, long iron tongs, in your hand. Keep *Gudri* and *Alphi.* Go to your palace as a *jogi* and beg alm from your mother sister and wife. Call your wife as *Bahna* or sister without any hesitation. Then only you have right to become a *Kanphata Sadhu.*

The Matt offered him Sadhu's dress. Bhartrihari dressed himself as directed by *Gorakh Nath*. He went to his mother's palace. She saw a resemblance of her son Bhartrihari in him but the *jogi* said, "She was a barren lady." After deceiving his mother he went to his sister's palace. She also saw a resemblance of her brother in him. He consoled her that she was the only child from her mother.

Bhartrihari, as a yogi, went for begging to his wife's palace and called her *Bahana* or sister. She recognised him but he said that she was widow by birth. His wife was not dissuaded by him. She put some questions and Bhartrihari replied them all.

Wife: Why did you tie *Kangna,* the sacred thread tied round the right wrist of a bridegroom-as your acceptance for marriage ceremony?

Bhartrihari: When I tied that thread Kangna, my inner self was weeping. I accepted that unwillingly.

Wife: Why did you put on *mor* or bridegroom-crown, on your head before proceeding for marriage to my residence?

Bhartrihari addressing his wife as Bahana or sister held out his *Jholi* or pouch for begging. This was an extreme test point of his life. He became a *pacca jogi.* He came to *Gorakh Nath* and placed the alm so begged before his Guru. He accepted him as his *chela* or disciple.

Bhartrihari wandered with his Guru from place to place. Many mutts are spread all over the country to preach his teachings. It is believed that both Bhartri and his Guru Gorakh Nath are still alive. They go from one place to other begging alms. Only a person with great vision can recognise them because they always move together.

❄ ❄ ❄

31. Eunches: The Looters

Shabnam and Shama were born in different states, different religions, different families and even different castes. But their oneness was that they belonged to one special category-eunuch. Shabnam was impotent man while Shama was a female singer. As eunuchs have no acceptability in the society right from birth are considered inauspicious and unlucky. Even their sight is ominous. So both of them were taken away from their families by the *Mausi* or the elderly eunuch. They did not know their parental heritage. All what they knew was that they were brought up among eunuchs and that was their natural family.

Both Shabnam and Shama learnt the art of singing and dancing. As they grew up they joined the party of singers and dancers. They accompanied the head of the party and went from street to street performing their art. Stylish clapping with twisting and stretching body parts was the special recognition of their party. Their most festive day was when they reached out a family where the male child was born. Like most unwanted guests they would picket in front of the home. They would sing and dance in jumping and busting style. They may even open the door of newly wed couple and newly born boy baby. Many families paid them the money and asked them to go but they would perform full dance-drama and then moved away by blessing the happy family.

Shama and Shabnam's dancing party was accompanied by the drum beater and a harmonium player. Some of them more good dancers. Shama would not hesitate to join marriage parties and become a Dulha or bridegroom. Shabnam will act as her groom. They would force the members of the wedding families to dance or twist with them.

One day a family used unbecoming words for party. Shama grumbled and said that they were the most unfortunate creature born on the earth. They were thrown away by their parents just after birth. Even their looks are taken as bad omen. Their party sit out side their door. They started weeping bitterly. Children from the nearby street gathered there. They imitated them. It was a big show for the village. The house holder was forced to give them some donation when they resorted to death-like mourning by beating their thighs and breasts.

Shama, Shabnam and their party were not satisfied with their earnings. They had to spend a lot of money on cosmetics. They had to wear goddy latest fashion dress to attract the men and women. They wore costly ornaments also. They had to deposit their daily earning with the *Mause* of their household.

Shabnam and Shama had heard that looters and robbers were earning a lot. The decided to form a band of dacoits and robbers. But they needed full dress of the robbers. They had to arrange some guns and knives, to act effectively.

They took permission from the *Mausi*. The Mausi was very wise. She warned them as they may be recognised by there way of talking and walking and clapping. They are accustomed for clapping on every occasion. Their way of clapping is very familias. More-over their inner built up is very woman like. They can roar but cannot face the uproar of the opponents.

Shama and Shabnam were bent up on carrying out their attempt. They arranged all equipments needed for the dacoity.

Now the question was to fix some time and place for this adventure. They allotted different roles to the band of so called dacoits. Shama was to give command to the band. Shabnam was to follow Shama. Other members of the band move to attack and collect the booty. They had some coloured shawl and veils which they got as gifts from the families to tie up the loot.

The time for dacoity by amateur dacoits was set just after sun set so that their facial features could not be recognised easily. All of them wore male dresses to look like dacoits. Shabnam wore black turban and covered her half face with a gaudy coloured handkerchief. He held a dummy revolver. The members of the band were also equipped with fake weapons.

The place of attack was a bushy corner near a small bridge. Every passerby had no alternative but this narrow bridge. A boat was kept in waiting to load away the booty. The band was also to sail in the same boat. Two eunches were to navigate the boat.

Incidentally they saw a man coming in a chariot accompanied by some followers. The chariot was jingling with small hanging bells. The 'dacoits' took it as a rich party. There must be some newly wed groom ladden with costly ornaments. They did not want to miss this chance for looting.

Shabnam challenged the charioteer to stop. Shabnam declared herself as a Kala Daku. She ordered them to handover the cash and ornaments to save their lives. The driver of the chariot counted the members of the band. They numbered a dozen. He was frightened. He conveyed the danger to his master who was sitting with his wife and baby boy. The lady was going to his parents after her delivery for the first time.

The charioteer belonged to a royal family. He was bold and fearless. How could he surrender without a combat. He came out of his chariot and stood on wooden yoke. He claimed, "O you *Hizras* or eunuchs! Runaway from my path. Make way for me. I am a prince. 'Hizras' cannot face me.

The prince used the word 'Hizra' without knowing their reality. It was a figurative use for important man. He wanted to low down the enemy through brave words. But Shabnam took these words in real sense. He thought that he has been recognised. Their 'Hizra' identity has been revealed. It took them no time to come to their true colours and reality. They clapped time and again saying. *Wah Sahib Khoobe Pahchane*'—O our lord we have all praise for you because you recognised us in reality. Some one has really said that nature cannot be hidden. And so they poor creatures were exposed completely.

Shabnam pulled down the gaudy handkerchief from his face. The prince recognised it. This was the same piece which Shabnam had snatched from his hand when she came with his dancing party on his son's birthday ceremony. The prince laughed heartily.

His wife lifted the veil of the chariot. She was surprised to see that a full band of eunuchs dressed like dacoits were dancing and singing around their chariot. The high drama of dacoity was changed into a dancing fete. The prince had met many "*Bahuroopyas*"—mimics or dissemblers—visiting their palace to demand or big money but facing eunuchs as mimics was his first experience. He never thought. That they were looters. He blessed them with some money and gifts.

Shabnam and Shama returned their home and offered their 'loot' to the Mausi. When the Mausi questioned the meager 'loot' they related the whole story to her. She clapped and laughed.

❄ ❄ ❄

32. For Whom to Pray

Ramu was a farmer. He had two daughters. He brought them up with great care. His wife Radha was a gentle lady. She took care of her daughters so that their future life will become happy. She engaged them in various household activities for practical training. For girls house itself is a practical laboratory. Both the girls took keen interest in home affairs.

The elder daughter named Sunahran took special interest in pottery. Right from her childhood she used to mould mud in different and beautiful shapes. She used to paint theme with local colours. She never sought anything from any lady still she was a good pot-painter. Earthen toys were her best friends. It was a complete world for her. Sunahran's girl friends joined her company for toys'-sake. She devised many games related to toys. One day Sunahran's mother saw her arranging the marriage between earthen toys. She told about her activities to her husband. Her husband decided to marry the daughter to some potter.

Ramu's younger daughter, named Phulan took interest in plantation. She used to plant saplings. She watered them properly. She was a keen plant designer. Phulan grew various types of flowers. Her girl friends came to her for flower-sake. Phulan turned the house into a beautiful nursery. Once she arranged marriage of a Tulsi plant with Saligram. Phulan's friends joined in singing songs. It was a big festive day for them. Her mother Radha told about Phulan's activities to her husband. He was happy. He decided to marry Phulan to some gardener.

As the daughters grew up he married the Sunahran to a potter and the younger Phulan to a gardener. Both of them lived happy lives.

One day Radha asked Ramu to visit their daughters to offer them some Diwali presents and to know about their well being. Ramu agreed and made all necessary arrangements.

First Ramu visited his elder daughter Sunahran. She had prepared earthen pots and set them out to dry. As the Diwali festival was nearing she prepared special earthen lamps, special worship pots and artistic toys. Her home gave a museum like look. All the members of her family were busy in preparing the kiln. These kachcha dry pots were to be cooked in the kiln. They had collected dung-cakes, straws and other necessary burning material. Kiln was to be arranged very skillfully so that all the pots were cooked well. Even a little negligence can prove too costly for them.

The father was happy to see that her daughter Sunahran was so hardworking. Her husband praised her art and skill. The father asked her daughter Sunahran for help from his side. The daughter said, "O father, you are a sacred man. Pray to God so that it may not-rain. Little rain can spoil our kiln. We will be ruined if it rains. Please always pray to Lord Indra not to shower at least for a fortnight. Our pots will be ready within that period. Sunahrans's father assured her for prayers.

Ramu's another daughter Phulan who was married to a gardener who lived not very far off. It was hardly six miles' walking distance. Instead of going back to his house he decided to visit for younger daughter Phulan directly.

Phulan was happy to see her father. She received her father's presents respectfully. Her children were happy to get sweets from their Nana or maternal grandfather. Ramu asked about her general well being. She looked sad. Her father became anxious. He put some probing questions about her gardening practices.

Phulan said, "Father, it did not rain this year. The fruit plants are generally dry. The flower nursery gave little flowers. We could not supply garlands and flowers to the marriage parties. We have little hope for rain upto Diwali. If it rains we can recover our loss by proper supply of fruit and flowers."

He listened Phulan's sad tale with full sympathy and said, "Dear daughter, what can I help you at present?"

Phulan said, "O dear father you are a sacred man pray to God for rain in this fortnight. If Lord Indra, the God of rain, is pleased we will celebrate our Diwali festival with full pomp and show, otherwise...."

Phulan's father was in a fix. He could not decide what to do. On one hand rain meant disaster for the potter's family and on the other hand it meant shower of wealth for the gardener's family.

He returned to his house. His wife Radha asked him about Sunahran and Phulan. He did not utter a word. Radha became sad. She again said, "Why don't you open your mouth? Has some one died in their family?"

Ramu said, "No body has died. But death like situation is about to arise to one of the family if I pray to God."

Radha said, "Praying to God never brings death or disaster. Rather it saves us from these sufferings. Pray, pray to God. Do not hesitate. What is the riddle in praying? Please reveal it."

Ramu said, "Sunahran needs no rain to save her kiln. She asked me to pray for no rain. Phulan needs rain for her garden to save it from draught like situation. We married our daughters to two different occupational families. You tell, should I pray? One of the family must suffer from my prayer. I leave it on God's will. Radha nodded helplessly.

❄ ❄ ❄

33. A Daana and The Caged Parrot

Once a Daana demon lived in a cave-palace. He was like a fiend. His fiendish acts were very horrifying. He ate man, woman and children. He hated mankind. Due to his fiendishness no one dared going near that cave-palace. It was believed that the cave-palace was protected by devilish spirits and wild inmates.

One day the Daana kidnapped a beautiful Rajkumari (princess) of a state. A Rajkumar (prince) of a neighbouring state was in love with her. When he came to know about the kidnapping, he decided to free her from the Daana's clutches. The Rajkumari's father, a Royal king, assured Rajkumar to marry her daughter to him if she is freed from that devil.

The Daana tried to allure the princess by showing off his wealth. He had seven *kothris* or small dark stores. Each one of them was filled with jewels, diamonds, pearls, silver, gold, platinum and costly studded ornaments. He took her to these dark-rooms glittering with dazzle of costly stones. To express his deep love to her he handed over the keys of these stores so that she could visit them at her own will and think herself the owner of that wealth. He never opened the eighth dark *kothri*. He always kept its key with him. The Rajkumari became suspicious. She wanted to know that secret. She tried to know that secret but the Daana always evaded and avoided that question.

One day the Rajkumari and the Daana were basking in easy-going mood. Reading the Daana's mood Rajkumari asked about the secret of eighth *kothri*. Unimagining any conspiracy the Daana told that the inner door of that dark room leads to a snakes'den. No one can surpass them. Next to snakes'den flows the river of boiling poisonous water. It is sure death to a trespasser. If some one passes by floating nearly stones on the water he will face the black scorpions and centipedes. Their sting is sure hellish death for his misadventure. They can only be killed by the spray of dried powder of the red chilies. Next to scorpions and centipedes hill is a beautiful garden. A golden cage hangs on a tree. There lives a biting parrot. In that parrot lies his life and death. If the parrot is killed by chance he will also die simultaneously. He feels very safe due to his tedious and evincing planning. Thus she should marry him to live a happy long life.

The Rajkumari became sad because she had no chance of getting freedom from the Daana's clutches. But the Rajkumar was bent on to search her out. He was a good explorer and good smeller. He smelt the Danaas foot prints and reached his cave-palace. It was mid day. The Daana was out for hunting. The Rajkumari was all alone. She was peeping through the window to pass her time. She located a man near the cave-palace. She waved her hands. The Rajkumar took it as a happy sign. They recognised each other. The Rajkumari dropped a rope through the window and the Rajkumar climbed up. She arranged food for him.

Rajkumari told him that the Daana is a cannibal. He hates men. All his activities are fiendish. The Daana will not spare him. He will eat him up. It is not easy to run away from this cave-palace. There is one way out. She would turn him into a big black fly. The Daana would not notice him. At night she would again turn him into a Rajkumar. They can live a happy life.

When Rajkumari noticed that the Daana has turned up she changed Rajkumar to a big black fly and sticked it on the wall of her bed room. The Daana smelt here and there. He said that her room smells presence of man. He is hungry. He wants to eat him. The Rajkumari replied that he could eat her up, as there is no man in her room. The Daana felt sorry.

Rajkumari turned Rajkumar to his original shape at night and when ever Daana was away from the cave-palace for hunting. After some days Rajkumar felt himself caged in the cave palace. He asked Rajkumari to flee away from Daana's clutches. One night—Rajkumari told him about the green biting parrot and Daanas life and death in it. Rajkumari arranged arrows and dry powder of red chilies for Rajkumar and explained him the whole strategy of killing the parrot.

One day when Daana was away for hunting Rajkumar marched for his adventure. First he faced black hissing cobras spitting venom all-around. They were happy to see the prey of their choice but he proved their dead enemy. He hunted them down by the showers of sharp arrows. They made way for him while wriggling and hissing helplessly.

As Rajkumar marched forward on his adventure he came across a river with boiling water. He lifted some heavy stones and pushed them on the surging waves. The stones formed into a bridge and he hurriedly jumped over the river.

Across the river, below the ditches, he noticed the bands of black scorpions and centipedes jumping and dancing to see their prey. It was a hellish sighs to look at. Rajkumar made it most hellish by spraying dry powder of red chilies from above. It was like a bolt from the blue. All of them were freed from their present lives within minutes.

Rajkumar passing his way over the scorpions and centipedes reached the final stage of his adventure. The parrot was hanging and singing with fragrant blows of the air. It was frightened to see a dagger in Rajkumars hand. Seeing his death nearer it began to flutter and began trembling.

On the other hand Daana was also frightened and he too staggered and trembled seeing his death nearing him. Immediately he started running at an unimaginable speed towards the parrot. He could hardly believe that any one could even approach the parrot. He sensed a conspiracy hatched against him by Rajkumari. It was she to whom he had revealed the secret of his death. She must be loving some one. It is her lover who wants to get rid of him by killing the parrot.

The Rajkumar saw Daana gushing towards him like a flying saucer. To keep the situation under control he slashed one leg of the parrot. As Daanas life was in the parrot. Automatically Daana's one leg fell down on the ground. He became lame. He was still running fast. Rajkumar cut the second leg of the parrot so that the Daana could not kill him. The Daana still rolled and crawled and tried to catch Rajkumar neck. Before Daana could touch his neck he cut the parrots neck with a jerk. Daana's neck was also separated from his body. Rajkumar had a sigh of relief. Rajkumari reached the scene. She hugged her lover the loving Rajkumar.

The news of Daana's death spread like a wild fire. All the area enjoyed that news. Rajkumar married Rajkumari. He got the seven *kothries* full with diamonds, jewels, silver, gold and costly diamonds as a reward. Rajkumar and Rajkumari lived a happy life for a long period.

34. Whose Wife is She

Once a draught-like conditions prevailed for many years in a certain area. The villagers were the worst sufferers. Four friends living in that area decided to leave the village for the city in search of some bread-earning jobs. They were all young.

One of them was a *Khati* or carpenter. He was very skillful in carving wood. He could make very costly and artistic articles from wooden blocks. The second one was a *Darji* or a tailor. He could sew costly wedding clothes for the bride. The third was a *sunar* or a goldsmith. He earned name in the area for moulding and casting charming ornaments. His craftsmanship was all praiseworthy. The fourth was a *Pandit* or a sorcerer. He knew the skill of infusing spirit or life in inanimates.

All the four friends had to cross a forest area. At night they had to stay in the forest. For their safety and security they decided to guard themselves turn by turn till sunrise. They decided their turn by drawing straws of different sizes. All the friends placed their belongings in a nearby cave.

The carpenter was to guard first. All the three friends had a sound sleep. The carpenter felt bored due to loneliness. To avoid slumber and to engage himself in some useful activity he started carving a log. Soon it turned into a beautiful young lady. He was happy to see his creation. He was so much fascinated by the wooden idol that he kissed it time and again.

The tailor was to guard next. The carpenter handed over his duty to the tailor. The other three friends had a deep sleep. The tailor felt boredom in the lonely place. To avoid slumber and to engage himself in some useful activity he decided to do some tailoring job. He noticed the idol of a beautiful young lady lying nearby. He tailored charming gaudy garments well becoming to that young lady. He was so much fascinated by that idol that he garlanded his hands around its neck.

The goldsmith was to guard next. The tailor handed over his duty to the goldsmith. All the three friends had a deep sleep. The goldsmith felt boredom in the lonely place. To avoid slumber and sleep and to engage himself in some useful activity, he decided to make some golden ornaments. He noticed the idol of a beautiful young lady well attired. It lacked full beauty without ornaments. He decided to prepare golden ornaments for it. The goldsmith laded it with glittering ornaments right from top of toes. He was so much fascinated by that well carved, best attired and golden laden beauty that he kissed and embraced it time and again.

The *Pandit* or the sorcerer was to guard next. The goldsmith handed over his duty to the *Pandit*. The other three friends had a deep sleep. The *pandit* felt boredom in the lonely place. To avoid slumber and sleep and to engage himself in some useful activity he decided to tell beads to perform devotions in early hours of the day. He noticed the idol of a beautiful lady. It was well attired and laden with golden ornaments. It was so life like that he decided to infuse life in it by his art of animation. He performed his art and the beautiful lady started smiling. The *Pandit* raised his hand to bless her. The *Pandit* was a bachelor like the other three friends. He thought of making her his wife. As the wild cock crew all the three friends were awakened. They saw the *Pandit* talking and laughing with a beautiful woman. All the three friends claimed their right on her. The lady became a subject of dispute among them.

They decided to settle their dispute through the king. All of them reached the king's court. The king handed over the matter to his counsellor. The counsellor asked them to place their claim turn by turn so that he could give his reasoned judgement.

The carpenter claimed that she deserved to be his wife because he carved her out of wood most artistically. He gave her physical shape. All the three have no claim on his property. She belongs to him and him alone. He kissed her for the first time. The lady saw the carpenter with affectionate love.

The tailor claimed that she was a naked beauty. He preserved her modesty by providing her the dress of a wedding bride. He saw her as a wedding girl for the first time. He garlanded his hands around her neck to possess her. She undoubted belonged to him alone. The carpenter should withdraw his claim on her. The lady saw the tailor with fraternal look.

Claiming the right of his wife on the lady, the goldsmith said that lady without ornaments cannot become bride. He offered her the wedding bangles. She accepted it from him. The real husband of a woman is he whose bangles she wears. She is her bride by all means. He has spent countless money on her ornaments. The carpenter and the tailor should surrender their claim in his favour. This would be a natural justice. He kissed and embraced her for the first time.

The sorcerer was listening to his friend's arguments most patiently. On his turn he claimed that who would like to marry a well dressed wooden idol laden with gold ornaments. It blessed the wooden idol with life by his animating skill. When she came to life she saw him first. She laughed and talked with him for the first time. She was about to accept me as her husband but the cocks started crowing and my friends were awakened. The cock spoiled the whole game. Now you give your own judgement. The king's counsellor asked them to appear before the king next day.

The king held his court next day. All the four friends and the lady appeared before the court. The king asked his counsellor to announce the judgement with full logic based on local rules and customs regarding marriage.

The counsellor bowed before the king and said:

The carpenter played fatherly role because he gave the wood a physical shape. He was a fatherly kin to the idol.

According to the local customs special wedding clothes or dress are provided by the parental and maternal uncle families. The tailor performed that role. While garlanding his hands around the neck of the idol he only performed maternal uncles duty and rite.

The *Pandit* or the sorcerer acted as a *Devta* or god who infused life in the wooden idol by his knowledge of animation skill. The sorcerer act of kissing and embracing amounted to blessings by elders. He cannot claim it as a lover's act.

The bridegroom's family provides ornaments to the bride. The bride wears the bangles in the name of her husband and wears it during her life time. His kissing and embracing act was a husband like duty. According to the judgement the goldsmith is the real claimant of this lady. All the three friends accepted the judgement. All present in the court praised the wise counsellor's judgement.

❄ ❄ ❄

35. Kalavati Versus Kamlapati

Once a King named Samar Singh ruled the hilly area around Aravali mountain. He married his son Veerapal Singh with a princess named Kamlavati. The couple was very beautiful but haughty by birth and traditions. Both were good shooters and riders. The stories of their repute spread far and wide.

One night a trouble broke out between the two. Prince Veerpal claimed that a man is always far superior to woman. He always surpasses her in the area of might, intelligence and valour.

Kamlavati said, "Being my husband I have all regards for you but a woman is an equal match for a man in all these areas. She could even surpass man under certain circumstances."

Veerpal was highly annoyed because Kamlavati was not submissive before him. He claimed that he would not like to live with such a woman who is so much proud and unsubmissive.

Kamlavati said, "let us live together and you can try your words in due course."

"Why in due course? Why not tomorrow roared Veerpal. Kamlavati accepted his challenge. It was decided that both of them would prove their worth during hunting adventure before the courtiers.

Both Veerpal and Kamlavati had a very restless night. Both were married recently. They had to tread a long path of their married life. But a strained life is worse than hell.

Two best equipped and decorated horses were placed at their disposal. The restless horses were scratching earth with their hoofs as a sign of invitation to their riders. Both Veerpal and Kamlavati jumped upon the saddles fixing their feet firmly.

Veerpal and Kamlavati were to hunt a lion. They spurred their horses. Their attendants were left far behind. Their horses were panting due to sun. At last they located a lion roaming in a grassy jungle. Veerpal lost no time in shooting an arrow on his prey. The speed of the arrow was so swift that it crossed the long hair of lion's neck but did not strike its neck. The lion just gave a jerk to its neck and moved on. Kamlavati had her chance for hunt down the best. She took out an arrow from the quiver and shoot it on the lion's head. It struck in the middle of its forehead. The lion fell dizzy and fainted on the ground. Veerpal took this strike on him and not on the prey. His lips were dried up. He swallowed the insult and consoled himself. But his inner spirit of manhood was pricking and pinching him.

Kamlavati smiled. She looked towards her husband and said, "Today I have openly proved that a woman is more powerful than man. In future I can prove that a woman is no less inferior than man intellectually. She can be superior rather. Let us close this topic and live a life on equal terms. Any ego can invite unlimited trouble for the family.

Veerpal felt rejected and dejected by this hunting episode. He decided to leave his palace and to settle elsewhere. He left the home for good to teach a lesson to his wife. A wife's separation from her husband is not less than death.

During his sojourn outside he faced many hardships. At last he reached Kusumpur, a kingly state. Princes Kusumkumavati of that state was very beautiful. She was unmarried because none could answer her three questions as condition for marriage.

Those who tried their luck for marriage and lost the bet were working in her palace as bonded labours. Veerpal also lost the bet and worked in Kusumkumavati's garden as a grass cutter.

Kamlavati was sorry for her husband. She felt his absence and decided to search him out from any part of the land. She rode on her horse and left the palace. She reached an inn. The owner of that inn was a *Bhathiyarin*, a lady inn-keeper. Kamlavati became her friend. During their talk she came to know about Kusumavati's repute and her bet for marriage. Kamlavati, as per her intuition decided to go Kusumpur. There was some chance that her husband may be there in search of livelihood.

Kamlavati decided to wear man's dress and to pose as a young man. She changed her name from Kamlavati to Kamlapati. She reaches Kusumpur in man's guise. Kamlavati, now known as Kamlapati, stayed in an inn. The *Bhatiyarin* of the inn was attracted towards 'his' beauty. Kamlapati tried to know in detail about Kusumavati's bet.

The *Bhatiyarin* told her that Kusumavati puts three questions before a challenger. She had two mares. They were very similar to each other in all respects. But one of them is the mother and the other is its offspring. The challenger is to tell which one of the two is mother. Kamlapati pondered upon this riddle. He scratched his head and lost in deep thinking. He closed his eyes. *Bhatiyarin* thought that during exercising his brain the young man must be feeling giddy. She brought a glass of cold water and sprinkled some drops on his face. Kamlapati opened his eyes as if nothing has happened with him.

Bhatiyarin thought if the first riddle was so disturbing for her why to tell the second? But Kamlapati insisted for the second question.

The *Bhatiyarin* told her that the princess has two wooden blocks. They are very similar to each other in all respects—may be it colour, size, smell and other qualities. The suitor of her hand was to tell which of them is a part of trunk and the which a part of the root. Their similarities have become a riddle to the challengers. The defeated persons are working on bonded labours in Kusumavati's domestic activities. Kamlapati again closed his eyes and the *Bhatiyarin* again sprinkled water drops on his face.

Kamlapati opened his eyes and said, "What is the third question which Kusumavati puts before her challenger?"

The *Bhatiyarin* said, "O beautiful prince, I feel pity on you. I do not want to put you in never ending difficulty by telling you the third riddle. Better you return your home and enjoy your life with your wife. *Chaakar* has to serve as a petty personal worker. It is hellish duty and that too under a snobbish woman."

Though the *Bhatiyarin* spoke on very low key note yet Kamlapati was bent upon opening any intricate knot. Seeing Kamlapati firm, unwavering and steadfast in his resolve *Bhatiyarin* revealed the third riddle in these words.

Among the couple who is more resolute He or She?
Who feeds a woman, her husband or merciful He?
Among the couple who is sharp-witted, genius and full of valour?
Before solving this knotty riddle, please be dead sure.

Kamlapati listened to *Bhatiyarin* with utmost care. He contemplated and gave a serious thought to each and every word.

Kamlapaty went to sleep and got up early in *Brahm-muhurt* (early morning time) which is the right time for contemplation, concentration and uttering solemn prayers before gods. He put these three question before his inner soul and a befitting echo answered them all. He thanked his gods and decided to appear before Kusumpur's court to answer the question framed by the princess.

Before going to Kusumpur's court Kamlapati was walking in a nearby garden. He met a person cutting the grass with tears in his eyes. Kamlapati wanted to share his grief. The grass cutter advised Kamlapati not to go before Kusumavati otherwise he will also meet the same fate. Once he too had a beautiful wife but he quarreled with her on some issue. Kamlapati recognised him though his hair were scattered, beard was grown and his health was failing due to slavish job. He was nobody else but her husband Veerpal Singh. Veerpal could not recognise her as she was wearing man's dress.

Kamlapati felt sorrow and decided to free him from that state. She side tracked him and moved to opposite direction. She was told by another grass cutter not to take that direction because Kusumavati was talking with her nearest and dearest grass cutter. Kusumavati had developed love during his captivity period for him. But according to the bet she could not make any advancement towards him.

When the king's court was set for work Kamlapati reached there and claimed to try his luck to marry Kusumavati by answering the questions. Kusumavati was also there. She was sharing the court's work. She was attracted to see Kamlapati. A special court was arranged next day for the question-answer session. Kusumavati's mother was also present. She was appointed to give her final judgement.

The two matching mares were brought before Kamlapati for discrimination. Kamlapti asked them to arrange a water tank for the mares. Both the mares drank water turn by turn. Kamlapati said the mare which took the first chance for drinking is the daughter mare while the other is mother mare.

The king asked Kamlapati to explain her logic for discrimination so that all present could be satisfied. Kamlapti said, the mother is always very considerate for her sons and daughters. She gave first chance to its daughter out of affection and love. She would be satisfied with the leftover water."

All including the captives were pleased to hear Kamlapati's reply. Kusumavati's mother gave her judgement in Kamlapati's favour. Kusumavati smiled for the first time after a long period. A ray of hope was there which troubled her heart.

Kamlapati was to answer the second question. He was to discriminate between the two wooden blocks. He again asked the court to fill the tube with fresh water. The tube was filled with water and the two similar wooden blocks were put aside on a table. Kamlapati observed them by turning them round turn by turn and finally placed them in the water tank. He noted their movement and their reaction in the water. Finally he took out one wooden block and said, "This is a part of trunk of the tree and the other belongs to the root part.

How could the court believe without proper logic behind his act of discrimination between the two. Kusumavati's mother asked him to explain his logic. Kamlapati again dipped the two wooden block in the water tube. One of them was floating and other dipped to the bottom side. Kamlapati said, "The root part of the tree is always heavier because being feeder part it remains under earth and transmits water onward. The trunk part is lighter because it remains in the air."

All those present, in the court, including all the captives, were satisfied with Kamlapati's logic and Kusumavati's mother gave her judgement in his favour. Kusumavati was also very happy.

The court was adjourned because Kamlapati asked for a week's time to answer the third question after proper tests and observations. He was allowed to stay in the palace as his marriage with Kusumavati was almost certain. The princess also met and chatted with him. Some attendants were also put at Kamlapati's disposal.

One of the attendants observed Kamlapati's while changing his dress. He developed some doubt that Kamlapati was a woman in man's wears. This news reached in the palace corridors. Kusumavati's mother talked to her husband. Her husband said that this doubt could be removed in the open field during hunting expedition. If he is woman he would bend forward to hide her breast otherwise he would sit straight. This expedition can be arranged tomorrow. The news of this expedition and the 'doubt' reached Kamlapati through his well wishers. During hunting Kamlapati showed his ability and the doubt was proved as most unfounded. Kusumavati's father was satisfied but her mother was still suspicious and asked for a second test.

As second test Kamlapati was to cook his own food with wet fuel. If he is a female he will bear all the troubles and if he is a male he will throw water in the hearth and will leave the kitchen in rage. Some servants conveyed this news and he successfully passed this test also.

One week's time was over. The open court assembled. All were happy because Kamlapati was expected to answer the third question after completing the couplet. The princess will be married to Kamlapati. They would enjoy the delicious dishes. The king, Kusumavati's father, read the couplet.

Among the couple who is more resolute, He of She?

Who feeds the woman, her husband or merciful He?

Among the couple, who is sharp-witted, genius And full of Valour?

Before solving this riddle please be dead sure.

Kamlapati replied:

Among the couple 'she' is more resolute And not 'he',
Fate feeds a woman neither her husband nor He.
Among the couple woman is sharp-witted, genius And full of valour;
I have practically solved your riddle
I am dead sure.

The court was surprised to hear such a bold judgement from a youngman's mouth. The queen approved his judgement by the nod of her head but the confusion and suspicion engulfed others. They thought that the queen approved the answer sheer out of love for her daughter and to end her frustration because the marriage of the princess was getting too late.

Confusion and suspicion continued in the gathering over queen's judgement. A captive who had a special liking for the princess was the most disturbed person. If the marriage is arranged she would go away to her in-laws. The princess had also a liking for that captive. Kamlapati knew it from the first day during her-walk in the garden.

The king asked Kamlapati to explain the logic behind his answer before the entire court. Kamlapati wanted a promise from the king that he would abide by his words. The king gave him words and full assurance.

Kamlapati said, "I accept Kusumvati as my wife. I have completed your couplet. She is very much mine. Now I hand over her to the captive whom she likes most. Both like each-other."

Everyone was stunned to hear Kamlapati. There was dead silence for a moment. Soon it turned into "whispering noise—The king asked Kamlapati the reason for not marrying the princess despite winning the bet.

Kamlapati said that she is a woman. Her name is Kamlavati and not Kamlapati. She had proved through her hunting adventure that a woman is full of valour. She has proved by her other test that a woman is sharp-witted and genius. None could recognise that she was a woman. Only queen had some doubts and so she gave her judgement in her favour. She queen is more intelligent than the king, her husband. A woman is not always dependent on her husband's earning. She earned her bread due to his blessing. All looked at each other's face.

Kamlavati again said that all the captives be released immediately. My husband Veerpal Singh is one of them.

Tears rolled from Veerpal's eyes. He stood up and felt sorry for the harsh treatment met to his wife. Kusumavati was married to the young man of her choice. Kamlavati and Veerpal Singh returned to their kingdom and lived a happy life.

❄ ❄ ❄

36. Ramlu and Dhapaan

Dhapaan was an old lady. She became widow in her teenage. Members of her family fell prey to some epidemic. She was the only fortunate or unfortunate lady to survive in the family. Social customs forbade her for a second marriage. Only few options were open for her to make both ends meet. In the harvest seasons she worked as a farm labourer. Otherwise she would grind grains for the rich families by *Hath-Chakki* or hand grinding mill because there were no flour-mills those days.

Whenever the face or upper and lower millstones of her *chakki* were worn-down or became smooth Fazarali used to roughen them by the strikes of a special hammer. But this time the *maani* or the wooden bush fitted in upper millstone became out of use. This was not harvest season. Dhapaan earned her bread only by grinding the grains. Those were auspicious marriage days. She was busy day in and day out on her grinding mill. But a minor defect in her *chakki* made her jobless. Moreover the pressure of the needy families tortured her mind and soul as she was losing her repute for doing work at right time. She was badly in search of some carpenter.

The elderly village carpenter was out of station for a week. But she could not afford to wait for so many days. The carpenter's son Ramlu was at home. He was not a perfect carpenter. He was an amateur or just a beginner. In the absence of his father he use to mend petty jobs here and there.

Dhapaan saw him carrying his tools on his head, well packed in a bundle. She had a sigh of relief. For her Ramlu was like a straw for the drowning man. When Ramlu shouted in the street for petty mending jobs Dhapaan immediately followed him with fast speed. Ramlu turned back and paid respect to *Taai* a respectful addressing term towards elderly ladies Dhapaan. She carried him to her home and showed the cracked *maani* or wooden bush fitted in the upper stone of the grinding mill. Ramlu assured her to mend the *maani.* She showered blessings on him and asked for the proper fee. Ramlu asked her to pay whatever she liked after the job is completed according to her best satisfaction. Dhappan felt satisfied.

Ramlu put the bundle of his tools on the ground and began to arrange them. His axe, chisel, small saw, *randa* or plane, hammer, screw-driver were all glittering because they were used very sparingly. Dhappan was satisfied to see his tools. Ramlu was all set for work.

Dhappan was in a hurry to fetch water from the village well to avoid the heat of the sun. The well was far away from the village on the bank of a pond. She put earthen pitcher, water drawing rope and a bucket on her head and said, "Ramlu, I am going to fetch fresh water for you from the well. You carry on your mending job. I shall pay your money on my return." Ramlu nodded his head while handling his tools.

Ramlu pulled out the *maani* or wooden bush from the *keela* or the large spike. It was cracked from the middle. He handled his tools carefully, as he was still a beginner he failed in his assignment. The *maani* prepared by him was a bit larger in size. He tried to fit it on the large spike with full force.

To his great surprise the upper mill stone developed cracks. He still hammered the *maani* to fit it in the large nail. The more he tried the greater and larger the crack became in the mill stone. At last the mill stone fell on the ground or the mud base, where the flour in stored. His hammer slipped from his hand and struck the mud base. The mud base was broken into pieces.

Seeing the unwanted loss Ramlu was confused. He was taken aback. He stood up abruptly in a gushing state. His head was struck by the *chhinkaa* or the hanging dazed basket. Dhapaan had stored, butter and curd on it in two small pots. Both the pots fell on the ground and were broken. Curd and butter were spilled on his newly tailored clothes. Poor Ramlu was to wear them next day to visit his father-in-law's house to bring back his wife. His game was spoiled.

Ramlu thought of cleaning the butter and curd immediately to avoid scars and stains from his clothes. He sat on a *chaarpai* or cot. The cot was old. Its strings and bamboo poles could not withstand his weight. They cracked and poor Ramlu fell down on the ground with a thud.

Dhapaan's goat was standing nearby. It was enraged and hit Ramlu on his back and tried to run away from the house. Ramlu tried to catch it by its rope. The goat hit him back with full force. Ramlu was struck against the door. The door cracked down and hit on Ramlu's shoulder.

It was a great loss for Dhapaan. The scene of broken *maani* cracked millstone, crumbled mud base, scattered butter and curd, broken cot and door was before his eyes. There was no alternative for Ramlu except to run away from the scene.

On the other hand Dhappan was getting late. She was worried for Ramlu must be waiting for getting his remuneration for the work perfectly completed long back. He must be getting late for his next job. He may be complaining against her. She tried to move fast.

To her great surprise she met Ramlu on her way back. She felt sorry. Ramlu looked disturbed. She tried to untie the knot of her *chunni* to pay him the money but Ramlu refused to accept. She moved forward to pay the money and Ramlu moved backward to avoid her.

In this sort of push and pull game Dhappan's foot struck against a stone. She stumbled. The earthen pitcher fell down on the ground. It was broken into pieces. Her clothes were soaked. Ramlu's clothes were already oily and greasy.

Due to loss of pitcher and old age Dhapaan became angry. She cried, "O Ramlu, how to bewail you and for how long (*O Ramlu tumhein Kahaan tak aur kab tak roun.*)

Ramlu replied in allegoric language—Bewail me upto your doorstep and inside your house and thereafter bewail for a long time (*Darwaze aur under tak der tak roote rahnaa.*) She could not understand Ramlu's statement but when she entered into her door and saw everything broken, she began to weep loudly repeating Ramlu's name and cursing him.

To save him from his father's rebuke Ramlu left his village. He only returned when he was master of his job. He compensated Dhappan though late and she withdrew her harsh words used by her in anger. Ramlu is still remembered in jokes in his area. His name has become a proverb.

❄ ❄ ❄

37. Teku: The Third Partner

Once there lived a rich *zamindar* or a landlord in a village. His name was Shivnath. He had a son. He named him Tekchand. Being son of a rich man he feared from none. Most of the time, he resorted to bad activities and misadventures. People were fed up with him but they were helpless.

Tekchand wanted to win name and fame may it be in good or bad sense. Once it rained heavily. He went to a nearby village at night. He drove away his cattle to his village pond and tied them with trees. It rained so heavy that the lowlying area of the pond side was overflooded and the cattles met a watery death. The villagers were surprised to see that havoc but no one could trace out the culprit. Tekchand's devil heart leaped with joy.

Tekchand's criminal activities knew no bounds. He raised a dacoit-band. Once in wedding season he planned a dacoity. The target was Ratan Lal goldsmith's shop. Many wedding parties had given gold to the goldsmith for preparing golden ornaments. The gold amounted to lac of rupees. Tekchand entered Ratan Lal's shop, looted gold at gunpoint and ran away with the booty.

The news of dacoity in Ratan Lal's shop spread like a wild fire. Dozens of families in the area were affected. Some even raised doubts on Ratan Lal's honesty. The goldsmith lodged a complaint with the police. The Police Inspector concluded that three persons were involved in the dacoity. Their shoes prints more clearly visible on the hearth-ash stored by the goldsmith in a corner.

The Police Inspector called the village cobbler for help in investigation. The cobbler was wonderstruck to see the shoeprints. He was in a great suspense. His finding could bring a slur on a respectable family. His own family could be in danger. He flatly replied that many people come to him and put orders for preparing their shoes. He could not tell exactly about those shoeprints. The Police Inspector said to Shivnath, the village *sarpanch*, to further investigate the matter. Where a high officer fails, local person can easily be successful. He pinned his faith on Shivnath and went away.

Shivnath personally went to Sanwalia, the cobbler Sanwalia was one of the *panchayat* members. Shivanath said, "I know the cause of your hesitation. You think that involving yourself in the case means visiting court many a time and losing your daily labour. It can be danger to your life. But being a *panch* you have your duties also. I will protect you by all means."

Sanwalia gained confidence. He revealed that the shoe-prints showed that one of the dacoit was Badan Singh, the village wrestler. Shivnath went to Badan Singh's house. Badan Singh was away to attend his younger sister-in-law's marriage. By nature also a thief leaves the place of accident to avoid hardship.

Shivnath informed the police. The Inspector accompanied by Shivnath and Ratan Lal reached Kota, the wedding place of Badan Singh's sister-in-law. All of them were disguised. There was hustle and bustle in the village. The ornaments to be presented to the bride were on display. All the villagers were praising Badan Singh for his generosity. The three outsiders also saw the ornaments. Ratan Lal had a full inventory of the ornaments made by him. He showed the list to the Inspector and compared the ornaments itemwise. They were exactly one third of the total lot or loot.

Badan Singh was arrested. All the looted ornaments were recovered from the site. There was confusion and panic in the village. Some *baraties* tried to intervene but Badan Singh confessed his guilt and left with the police inspector.

The Police Inspector tried to know about the two absconding culprits. He tried his best to know their names from Badan Singh. Badan Singh resisted. But even ghosts fear before thrashing. He told them that Padam Singh was his accomplish. Padam Singh was a fearful name in the area. It was only Badan Singh who could name him. His dark complexion, long twisted moustaches, big mole on his fleshy cheek and roaring voice presented him like *yamaduta*. Even the Police Inspector was shaken when he heard his name. But Shivnath and Ratan Lal were confirmed witnesses with him.

Putting Badam Singh behind the bars all the three tried to find out Padam Singh's whereabout. They came to know that Padam Singh had gone to his sister to attend a wedding ceremony of her daughter. He is there as a *Bhatai* to make presents to the bride. They went to the village magra, the wedding place. The *Bhat's* articles brought by *Bhatai,* Padam Singh, were on display. All the villagers were praising Padam Singh for his generosity. The ladies were singing songs. They were counting the ornaments in their songs item wise. All the "three outsiders" were listening the songs attentively.

The Police Inspector raided the room where the gift articles, including ornaments, were on display. There was hustle and bustle all around. Ratan Lal had a full inventory of the ornaments made by him. He showed the list to the Inspector and compared the ornaments itemwise. They were exactly one third of the total loot or lot.

All the ornaments were recovered from the site. There was confusion and panic in the village. Some villagers tried to intervene but Padam Singh confessed his guilt and left with the Police Inspector.

The Police Inspector tried to know the third accused and the remaining part of the ornaments. Neither Badan Singh nor Padam Singh revealed the name of the third partner of dacoity. The Inspector inflicted harsh torture on Padam Singh but he did not open his mouth. When Shivnath went to meet Padam Singh in jail he was surprised to see that every part of his body was swollen. He felt pitty on him and got him discharged on bail. He arranged best treatment for him and gave human touch to console him.

After ten or fifteen days Shivnath consoling Padam Singh said, "You have borne harsh torture at the hand of the police. Why do not you tell the truth? What is the pressure upon you? Heaven will not fall if you reveal the truth."

Padam Singh said," *Sarpanch Ji,* opening my mouth means bringing slur on a respectable family for generations to come. I shall suffer jail but not open my mouth".

Shivnath said, "both of you have hatched some deep conspiracy. You again resolve yourselves the matter. I shall arrange your meeting in the jail." Both of them met but nothing came out.

Shivnath did not accept his defeat. Justice is uppermost in the eyes of a *Sarpanch.* One day he called Sanwalia and said, "Sanwalia, I have given word to *Inspector Sahib* to unearth the truth. Our *Panchayat* should not cut a sorry figure in this case. On your little hint police caught two accused. Only you and you alone can open the next intricate knot. Both of them are the chips of the same block. The respect of entire *Panchayat* is at stake. My personal respect will also ruin."

Sanwalia said, "*Sarpanch sahib,* your respect is at stake in both the ways. It stands a high chance for its ruin if the truth is revealed."

Sanwalia's words were stinging Shivnath like a snake. He said, "Sanwalia, do not weigh my respect. Give weightage to Panchayat."

Sanwalia said, "Are you so much convinced?" "Yes I am", said Shivnath.

"Tekchand," Sanwalia said.

"Takchand", repeated Shivnath.

"Yes Tekchand. I established his presence on the first day by his shoeprints," said Sanwaila.

"But you are too late. Tekchand will get the same punishment as his two accomplish. He is the third partner. I shall add the word "*Tihai*" or third partner as a slur with his name. He will be known as *'Teu Tihai.'*

Tekchand was bent upon spending the entire loot. He was a dead drunk. In an intoxicated state of mind he was on a gambling spree. He took out the bag containing stolen ornaments. On every move he put one ornament on stake. When last ornament was lost he had a sigh of relief and said, "Easy come, easy go."

Shivnath called a meeting of the *Panchayat*. He announced that my son Tekchand was a party in looting Ratan Lal's shop. Please help me in searching him out.

Hearing this stunning news two sympathisers sided Tekchand and said, "Sanwalia wants to malign your name due to coming elections. He wants to become *sarpanch* by downgrading you. We shall not accept his malicious allegation."

The wordy fight took an ugly turn. Shivnath said," Poor people and innocent children are more nearer to truth. Sanwalia is free from greed and attachment. Tekchand is not dead but alive. He is sure to return when the ill earned money is totally spent. I will present him before this *Panchayat*."

Tekchand returned next day. His father welcomed him with full patience as if nothing has happened. After bath he accompanied him to the worshipping room. He placed some drops of Gangajal-river Ganges sacred water on his right palm and said, "This Gangajal is in your hand. I will ask you a question. Do not tell a lie. Speak the truth or you will become a leper."

Tekchand never imagined that his father would entrap him in such a soft but fast net. Hearing the word 'leper' he shivered and spoke truth and nothing but the truth.

Shivnath was overjoyed. He immediately called a *Panchayat* meeting. He announced that. Tekchand had confessed his guilt. All the *Panchayat* members were stunned. Shivnath patted Sanwalia's back time and again.

When Police Inspector knew this news he came to the village. He congratulated Shivnath, the village *Sarpanch* because he searched out the truth without spending any money. He said, "Your *chhoti Sarkar*, the lower court has won and our *Bari sarkar*—higher court-has failed"

Shivnath paid the third share of fine and loss as his son was a third partner in dacoity and handed over Tekchand to the police. What was the punishment imposed by the court is not known to us. What people still know is that he bears the spur of "*Tihai*" or the third partner with his name.

❄ ❄ ❄

38. Dhanvati Redeems Husband

Once there was a merchant. His name was seth Munnamal. His business flourished due to his dedication and enterprise. His name became proverbial due to his richness and philanthropic nature. In his business activities he was helped and advised by his *Munim* or book-keeper. *Munim* Sahumal was very faithful and trustworthy to the family. Seth Munnamal had a son. His name was Pannamal. Munnamal loved his son because he was born after long prayers before Gods and Goddess in his late age.

Due to old age Seth Munnamal was seized by endless sickness. At last he was on his death bed. He said to his *Munim* Sahumal, "I amassed my property with hard labour. It should not go waste in the hands of my beloved son Pannamal. He should know the art of learning. Please handover the keys of my treasury to him only when he may earn one thousand rupees by his own efforts. Tell my son to go for earning in shade and return home only after shade. *Munim ji* gave him full assurance and he left peacefully to his next abode.

Munim Sahumal conveyed Seth Munnmal's last wish to his son. Pannamal was happy to know that his father loved him so much that as a last advice he asked him to avoid the heat of the sun. While going out for earning he would make all proper arrangements to be in shade. He got covered streets and main roads by canopies to move in shade. About a dozen attendants holding umbrella and parasol followed him.

In few days a large sum of money was spent from the treasury. Sahumal was worried. He told Pannamal to know the real and deeper meaning of moving in shade. Moving in shade for earning means to leave one's house before sun rise under stars' shades, and to return after sun set when the stars again appear in the sky.

Pannamal was convinced by long persuasion from the members of his family. He removed the coverings and canopies and sold it in the market. He claimed that money as his personal earning and demanded the keys of the treasury from Sahumal. Sahumal did not agree with him. He asked him to go out elsewhere for earning the money.

But before his departure Sahumal arranged his marriage so that, he may return home for his wife's shake. The name of his wife was Dhanvati. Pannamal left home with full determination to return after earning one thousand rupees. He went to a city. He worked as a labour and loaded heavy load on his head. His hair began to fall. He spent what little money he earned after hard labour.

He left that job and moved to other. There was a very rich oil-merchant. He had many *kohlus* (crushing oil-mills) to get oil from mustered seeds. The merchant was always in great need of *kohlu* drivers. It was a hard job.

To enslave or to make them as bonded labour he arranged certain tricks. He had a three storey *Haveli* or Building. It was very beautiful and attractive. No one was allowed to enter in it. On the roof of every story a beautiful peacock was set in a nest. The peacocks looked very real. It looked that they will just produce *peehu-peehua* shrill. Any one who could make the three peacocks to make a shrilling cry simultaneously would get that building. He would marry his daughter with the winner.

Many people who knew about the behaviour of the birds tried their luck. Some of them were even able to produce shrills either from one or the other peacock but all the three never shrilled simultaneously. All the betters became the merchants bonded labour and drove the crushing mills.

Pannamal in his childhood had also learnt birds cooings, chirpings, howlings, hootings and shrillings. He also tried his luck just out of frustration to become a multimillioners overnight but miserably failed. He too joined the crushing mill-drivers band.

He used to get up early in stormy nights and worked upto sun-set when the stars again appeared in the blue sky. Millions of mustard seeds were filled in the mills and by night all of them were spent up.

One day Pannamal missed his wife very much. He could not sleep that night. He decided to drop her a letter next day. Pannamal wrote in his letter that he earns millions everyday but all of them are spent up by night. His job is very soft. His simple duty is just to sit on his seat and to go round and round. He would return someday by saving the required amount.

When the letter reached his wife she sensed something foul in the message. She decided to search her husband out. Dhanvati changed her name as Dhanpati and put on man's dress. After some days she searched him out. He was poorly dressed. His hair were falling. He rarely took bath. From a shinning Panna Or precious stone was changed to a *peetal-adhanna* or a brass coin equal to three paise. But Dhanpati tried to search out some suitable job but remained unsuccessful. Some one suggested him to become a partner with the rich oil merchant. Dhanpati approached Telumal, the oil trader. Telumal was attracted towards the young beauty and his soft offer. Soon they developed intimacy and she lived with Telumal's family.

During Dhanpati's stay with Telumal two or three persons tried their luck to shrill through the peacocks but became bonded labours. Dhanpati wanted to know the mystery. Firstly the models of peacocks cannot shrill. Secondly how all the three peacocks can shrill simultaneously. It was a big question mark.

As Dhanpati's intimacy grew deeper and deeper her movement in Telumal's house became free from all restrictions. She noted a boy entering in the restricted area early in the morning and leaving by night. One day Telumal's family was out for some marriage party. She was alone in the house. She entered the room in the *Haveli* and tried to understand the mystery and finally she got success.

Dhanpati was in search of a person who would produce peacock's shrill and got success. Dhanpati whispered in his ears and he agreed to act according to the guidance. One hundred rupees were enough reward for him.

Next day a young man came to try his luck for Haveli and Telumal's daughter. Dhanpati got success in smuggling in the man who was to shrill like a peacock in Telumal's house. The boy who used to sit in the room and produced peacock's shrilling also jumped down from ceiling-hole. The man appointed by Dhanpati gagged the boy. The new entrant picked up all the three pipes filted with the models of the peacocks and started producing peacock's shrilling sound. All the three peacocks produced their sounds simultaneously. The new entrant went on producing shrilling sound continuously for a long time. It was just like siren. All the captives left their work and surround the building. Children and people surrounding the area gathered there. It was a big-big surprise show. Poor Telumal fainted.

He was to be exposed soon by Dhanpati. The man who was hiding in the Haveli and producing a peacock's shrilling came out. He explained how the three peacocks shrilled together. The gagged boy was freed.

Telumal came to senses. He freed all the captives or his bonded labours and felt sorry for his act of cheating. Pannamal was also a free man. Telumal gave his daughter to the winner. He was very happy.

Dhanpati asked Pannamal to return to his home but he expressed his inability. He can return only after earning one thousand rupees otherwise his *Munim* will not handover to him the keys of the treasury. Dhanpati offered him to pay the amount if he could give some articles possessd by him. Pannamal had only two utensils and two rags. One for bedding and other for covering. Dhanpati took utensils and rags in her possession and paid him the amount. Pannamal was overjoyed. It was a redeem day for him.

Dhanpati again became Dhanvati. She returned home. She claimed before the family that her pilgrimage was very successful. As blessing she may get her husband soon. All welcomed her and prayed for her husband's return.

It was a *Purnima* or full moon day when Pannamal returned home. His home gave a festival look. Special sacred *Satyanarain Katha* was arranged. Panamal handed over one thousand rupees as his earnest earning to *Munim ji*. *Munim* Sahumal handed over to him the keys of the treasury.

Pannamal and Dhanvati met at night. Pannamal boasted how he earned lacs and spend them by night. He claimed that one thousand rupee was not a great amount for him. He lived a very lavish life. It was her love which called him back.

Dhanvati smiled and smiled. She got up from her bed. She took Pannamal's hand in her hand and led him to a corner. Pointing towards two rags and two utensils she said, "This is my earning in your absence. Their cost is one thousand rupees."

Pannamal connected all the threads of the story and felt ashamed. Dhanvati forgave him and they lived a happy life for a long time.

❄ ❄ ❄

39. Tailless Serpent

About two hundred yards away from the village was a *Tila* or a mound. Villagers related many stories with it. Some related it to the remains of a *peepal* tree. Other related it to a man who could not pay his debt and there *deemak* or white ants are eating him up as a revenge and punishment. They are recovering their debt. Some still took it as *Bambis* or snakes holes. It was believed that a beared and winged snake still lived there. It bears a sandal *tilak* or mark on its forehead. People worship that hole like a sacred temple. They offered milk to the snake on certain days and occasions. This snake fulfills wishes and desires of the devotees.

Seth Kundan Dass was a faithful devotee of this snake-hole. He used to offer milk to the snake but the snake never tried to know his devotee's wish. Kundan was true to his word and he was never disappointed.

Once Kundan had a dream. He saw that a son was born in his house after fifteen years of worship. He offered his son to the snake. The snake was protecting him under his expanded hood. When he opened his eyes nothing was visible.

Next day he again offered milk to the snake-hole. He was on fast that day. At night Kundan saw a dream. He saw a long white bearded man. The man said, "I am pleased with you. Your desire for a son will be fulfilled. You will find a *mani* or precious gem and a *dori-sota* or rope and staff near the hole. Cross the sea with *mani's* help. Treat the enemy with *dori-sota*. You will face many difficulties. Amid the sea lives a *Rajkumari* or a princess. Bring sand touched by her feet and paste it on your wife's womb. You will get a son after nine months."

Seth Kundan opened his eyes. He went near the snake-hole. He found there a *mani* and *dori-sota*. He was so much overjoyed that instead of coming home he marched on for long journey for three months.

His wife was disappointed. People talked about lot of true-false stories. Some suggested his wife a second marriage. But she refused and fixed her eyes on the path from where her husband went and prayed for her husband's return.

Despite all odds he touched the sea's shore. His longing for the son was far higher than the waves of rising sea. He implored before the sea and said, "O sea god, you blessed this world with fourteen-*ratnas* or precious gifts. Please bless me with a son."

After bowing prayers he entered the sea. The *mani* made way for him amid waters. When he had gone deep he located a beautiful palace. There was dead silence. No one lived there—neither birds nor animals. Only some fish were visible in water ponds. He was deadly tired and went in to deep slumber.

When he opened his eyes he saw a beautiful lady by his side. She was Rajkumari Minakshi's maid servant. Her name was Meenakumari. He was frightened to see the maid servant. Meena smiled and said, "Why have you invited your death by coming here? The Rajkumari will eat you up. Don't you see that she has eaten even birds and animals of this area. I too, am hungry. I eat only three fish."

Seth Kundan Dass thought, Why not to feed her with best dishes. She will be faithful to me after testing my saltiest dishes." Kundan ordered his *Kundi-sota* to bring best dishes for Meenakumari. All the dishes were present in the twinkling of an eye. Meenakumari's mouth was watered and she enjoyed all dishes to her full.

Meenakumari asked Kundan the reason for his adventure. He told her that he needs sand touched by Rajkumari's feet.

Meenakumari told him that she always walks on velvet carpets. She never puts her feet on earth. How can he get sand touched by her feet?

Kundan requested that only she could help him in finding some way out. He knows nothing about that surrounding. Meenakumari said, "I am leaving this place. Other maid servant will be on next duty. It will take me some time to find out some solution. If you are saved I shall talk to you again."

The next maid servant knitted her illusory world around the area. Kundan Seth felt as if he was being haunted by hounds. Kundan remembered snake-god and took out his *dori-sota*. Within no time all the hounds looked wrapped in the rope. It looked as if they were being hit by the staff. To pacify the surrounding Kundan ordered *dori-sota* to stop their action.

The maid servant resorted to her second illusory magic. She turned herself into a beauty lady and hypnotized Kundan by her anormous tricks. She begged *dori-sota* and Kundan obliged her. In very next moment Kundan fell unconscious. When he came to senses he remembered snake-god most sincerely and as a result received back his weapons *dori-sota*.

Before going to sleep Kundan requested *dori-sota* to arrange some extra-ordinary gathering so that Rajkumari may come out to join it. It was a co-incidence that a full moon night fair was arranged in a nearby island. Rajkumari expressed her willingness to join the fair. She decided to have a bare footed walk amid beautiful and fragrant flowers. Meenakumari informed Kundan about Rajkumari's desire. But how it was possible for Kundan to enter ladies gathering?

Meenakumari offered her service. She picked up some sand touched by Rajkumari's feet and handed it over to Seth Kundan. Poor Meenakumari forgot that who so ever would pick up sand touched by Rajkumari's feet will become sick and die soon. As Meenakumari began to faint but Kundan saved her with the help of his *dori-sota*.

Seth Kundan returned home with precious sand but he was told that his wife Rupa waited for him for a long time. She offered milk on the snake-hole. Once she was kidnapped by the dacoits and nothing is known about her well being. Kundan asked help from his *dori-sota*. They beat the dacoits and freed her from their confinement.

Rupa was happy to see her husband alive. Seth Kundan felt sorry that he did not inform his wife about his adventure. He applied that precious sand on Rupa's womb. She gave birth to a beautiful son. They named him Naagdutta wich means received through serpent's blessing.

Nagdutta grew up soon. He used to go to snake's hole to offer milk daily. In return he daily found a *mani* out side the hole as a gift. Naagdutta became rich. Seth Kundan was happy.

One day the father and son hatched a conspiracy to kill the snake so that they could get the *mani* treasure once and for all.

Naagdutta went to the snake-hole. He placed the milk bowl with hole. He hid himself behind a tree with a long stick in his hand. As the snake came out to drink milk Naagdutta struck him forcefully with his stick. Its tail was cut. The furious snake jumped and stung Naagdutta on his forehead. He became blind. His body became blue. His father supported him but he breathed his last in his lap.

At night the same old white beard man appeared before him in his dream. The old man said.

I blessed you with a son at my own cost,
Still you stung by your avarice, behaved like a ghost.
I will remember the loss of my tail
Till my last breath,
Your son's horrible death with my sting
You will never forget.

❄ ❄ ❄

40. Rajhans and Beena

Once there was a man in a village. His name was Ghamandi. He had to work hard to make both ends meet. He had a large family. Despite hard labour his family lived from hand to mouth. Once his wife Beena suggested him to go to some city and start some pretty business. His wife was very beautiful. She was fond of playing *Veena*. Generally a man having a beautiful wife becomes suspicious towards her. Ghamandi did not like to leave his wife alone. But circumstances forced him to go out for a better earning.

Ghamandi started a *Panwari* or betel-leaf shop. He had a good earning. He sent a part of his earning to his wife. She looked after the family affairs and the children. She was busy throughout the day.

In the evening she used to play *veena* instrument for her own entertainment. It was a good past time for her.

Her *Veena* recital was very sweet and attractive. It looked as if the trees and the creepers were thrilled by the musical waves. There was a mango tree in her backyard. This mango tree bore extra shoots and flower-buds. The blossoms were so fragrant and inviting that bees and butterflies always hovered over it. The tree became extra shady and birds of various varieties settled on it. They expressed their joy by producing charming and sweet notes. It looked that they tried to be in tune with her *Veena* recital.

Fortunately a *Raaj-hans* or flamingo happened to fly over her house. It was fascinated by the charming *Veena* recital. The fragrance of new buddings and flowers added additional charm for it. It settled down on a shady branch. It looked as if boughs bowed down to give it a deserving welcome. The *Veena* strings resounded with extra sweet sound. The echo system all around was so perfect that Beena lost in her recital. It looked as if the music knews no ending.

When Beena was fully satisfied she gave rest to the strings. There was tranquility all around. The heavenly consoling silence was broken by a drip. Beena's concentration was broken by that dripping sound. She looked towards the mango tree. She was surprised to see a mooti or a sparkling pearl on the grassy ground. She picked it up and looked towards the tree. She was astonished to see that a *Rajhans* was perched decorating the branch of a tree. Beena bowed before it and uttered some welcoming ceremonial words to give it deserving respect. It fluttered as if it was responding her actions. This was their first intimacy.

Rajhans flew away to *mansarovar,* the most sacred lake on the planet earth, to swallow pearls. The sweet notes of Beena's *Veena* recital were still thrilling its ears. It picked the most precious pearl in its beak and flew back to Beena's residence to rejoice sweet notes. It wanted to present that pearl to Beena not as a fee but as a token award.

For days together it was *Rajhansa's* routine to fly back to *Mansarovar* and pick up a pearl for Beena. Their friendship grew so much that it will sit in Beena's lap and enjoy the music without knowing that too much nearness can bring trouble for both of them.

Beena became rich. She spent that money in constructing a decent bungalow and its interior decoration. A separate lawn and a beautiful lake was arranged for the guest, friend or the daily visitor—the majestic *Hansa.*

After some years Ghamandi thought of returning to his native place. He picked up his bag and luggage and reached his home. He was surprised to see a decent bungalow in place of an ordinary hut. Many doubts arose in his mind. The main doubt was that his wife had arranged a second marriage. Beena was standing in the balcony of her bungalow. She waved her hand with best respect and welcomed him. The bag and baggage brought by him was not compatible with that residence. It was placed in the outer corner.

Beena did not tell her husband the source of her income. Ghamandi did not ask about it. He himself would see and face the realities.

Beena sit on her *Veena* recital as usual. Her husband joined the company. He enjoyed the consoling music. The visitor *Rajhans*—did not notice the new visitor, Beena's husband. And why should it notice it. Its first and foremost motive was to enjoy the music. As routine he dropped a pearl and flew away. Beena picked up the pearl and put it in her purse. Ghamandi noticed it. He thought that her lover is hidden some where and he has made this offering as a token of appreciation. He noted that Beena sit for *Veena* recital at a fixed time and her lover throws a pearl from some hidden place. Due to his presence he did not appear in person before her. He decided to do away with the hidden lover.

After a week Ghamandi noted some fluttering sound amid his mango tree. But it was some bird. But a lover can be a disguised deceiver. This villain may be a cheat. He must be knowing the art of metamorphosis. He should be taught a lesson. Why should he reveal his doubt to his wife? She may become a party to him and may hatch a conspiracy. To a shrewd lady a lover or paramour is dearer than her own husband. Ghamandi was burning with jealousy.

Ghamandi arranged an arrow and bow. The *Rajhans* came as usual. Beena started the *veena* recital. Both Beena and *Rajhans* were lost in the world of music—calm, serene, soothing, otherworldly. Ghamandi's jealousy, suspicion, capriciousness were playing just an opposite note. The husband and wife though knotted together at the time of marriage were poles apart. Ghamandi shot an arrow on *Rajhans*. It fluttered. A fountain of blood flew poured downward. The *Rajhans* jumped and flew to Beena's lap. Being an innocent creature its groaning voice was complaining:

> You gave me a call
> Through musical notes
> You hid my enemy
> To give me deadly shots.

Little did the *Rajhans* know about a man's suspicious nature. Beena could not tolerate the false allegation. She too died with *Rajhans* claiming that she was chaste, trust worthy and innocent.

❄ ❄ ❄

41. Sweat Soaked Quilt

Baau was a quick witted fellow. He had to go to different villages to convey marriage dates fixed by either groom or bridegroom party. He had to deliver presents such as *Kurta-Topi, Peelia, Sindhara, Chhuchhak* and the like as per local traditions and customs on certain occasions on behalf of the parents or *jajman's* relations. He had to take local sweets like *Kothli, Kasaar, Khaand-Kasaar Suhali*. Some times he was over loaded with articles. He had to take rest on his way to the *jajmaan's* villages. On certain local occasions like marriage,

Sagaai, Lagan, Kaaj, Dishautan, and the like he enjoyed feasts and got money as per prevailing customs which ranged from *chavanni* (four annas) *Sawarupya* (quarter and one rupee) to eleven rupees. During these visits he had to drink water from different villages. He came in contact with numberless old and young people. "Baau" was a famous name in the area. You just name him and people will laugh recollecting his jokes and unusual behaviour.

It was difficult for him to carry his bedding and especially in winter season. The load of clothes and sweets was sufficient for him. Those days there were no buses and *tangas* conveyance between villages. There were no *pacca* roads. One had to carry loads on one's head only. Baau was willy nilly provided bedding by the family visited by him. He was generally given used, tattered dirty clothes not in use by members of the family. Though born in a poor family he was very fond of wearing good clothes. He generally shun the bedding provided by the family and stayed with some known relatives or friends.

Once it was winter season. On *Makar Sankranti* festival he had to carry presents to some *jajman's* relation. There were cold days. He asked a better quilt to save him from biting cold. An old lady gave him an old tattered, worn out and torn out quilt. Even stars could be seen through it. Baau asked for its replacement. The old lady snubbed him. The relationship was such that to keep and preserve their honour he kept mum. The old lady did not give weightage to his silence. She said, "Baau, this quilt will give you so much warmth that you will be soaked in sweat." Baau first laughed and left for a friend's house to spend that night. He placed the quilt given by the old lady in a corner. He slept in a good bedding provided by his friend.

The old lady's behaviour was troubling him. He wanted to give a befitting reply to her. Before going to sleep a wonderful idea struck in him mind. He had a hearty laugh on that idea. His laugh disturb the sleep of his friend. When his friend asked him the reason for laughing he postponed it for the next day.

Next morning Baau woke up as usual. He went out side in the fields to ease himself. He came to the village pond. He was carrying the quilt provided by the old lady. Baau always had a staff in his hand to avoid dog bite and cattle menace. He removed the quilt. He drenched it in the pond water and hung the quilt on his staff giving it his shoulder's support.

Baau went to the old lady's house and knocked at the door. The old lady came out from the house. Baau tried to hand over the soaked quilt to the old lady. The old lady was surprised to see that water drops are dripping from the quilt. She said, "O you naughty Baau what have you done? Why water drops are dripping from the quilt. It is so costly and you have spoiled it."

Baau promptly reacted, "*Mausiji* they are not water drops. There are sweat drops. This costly quilt gave so much warmth at night that I was badly perspired. Sweat drops began to drip from my body. I had to clean them time and again. During that struggle it became soaked due to excessive sweat."

The old lady simply grinded her teeth. Baau told his trick to his friend and both had a hearty laugh.

❄ ❄ ❄

42. A Long Bearded Woman

Tidda was an uncouthed, ignorant and unmannered man. His way of walking was like a Tidda or a grasshopper. His wife more or less bore the same characters and habits. So she was called Tiddi (a female grasshopper). They used to sell milk in adjoining township. Tiddi played an active role in animal *rearing* and buffalo milching.

Animals are accustomed to their master's way or touching. They sense the smells of their master's body and especially of their clothes. Tiddi used to milch her buffaloes. Her hands, palms, thumbs and fingers were very soft. While milching the buffaloes they enjoy the sense of touch of her thumbs and fingers. They have become *haathal* or accustomed to her hands for milching. They would never allow any other to touch their udders and teats. They even sensed the way of sprinkling water on udder for washing. As a result it was difficult for Tiddi to leave her house even for a day. She missed so many weddings of her relatives.

But once it was most essential for Tiddi to join in her younger niece's wedding. She had to perform certain ceremonial formalities. It was unavoidable for her. But how to carryout milching routine was a problem.

Tidda was a very simple and innocent man. He suggested to his wife Tiddi, that he would wear her clothes for milching the buffaloes.

The buffaloes would not recognise him for he would put veil on his mouth. He would grind the millstone by wearing her clothes so that the fresh smell of the flour may remain in the clothes and the animals have the same old feeling.

Tiddy went for joining the wedding after milching the buffaloes in the evening. She made all the necessary arrangement for the next day so that Tidda, her husband, may not face any difficulty.

Tidda wore his wife's dress *odhni-ghaghri*—early in the morning. But he could not find out the *chat* or the licking saltiest flour for the animals. He knew that his wife used to mix licking mixture in the flour so that the buffaloes enjoy it and yield more milk. So he sit on the stone mill to grind some flour.

A *jogi* from the village temple used to come to beg flour in the early morning when the women were grinding the flour. Raghunath jogi gave a call on the door. Tiddi used to offer a handful flour to Raghunath on his very first call. But for Tidda this was a novel experience. Raghunath jogi called thrice in a loud voice—O mother offer me some flour in the name of Niranjan. Tidda heared his call. He stood up and came out with handful of atta or flour. As Tidda was not accustomed to wearing woman clothes he forgot to hide his mouth under a veil. Raghunath jogi noticed a long beared woman. In the darkness of night Raghunath was frightened. As Tidda extended his hand toward his *Kothla* or begging bag he ran away shouting "bhoot-bhoot-bhoot" or a ghost. The flour spread over the ground. Tidda realised his mistake and felt ashamed.

Raghunath made an out cry in the street. Some neighbours came out. Raghunath made full description of the beared ghost in woman's dress. People made fun of Raghunath and did not believe him. Some women doubted when they saw the flour scattered on the door step. But the matter was silenced because people had to carry out their own household routine in the morning.

Tidda went out to his cattle enclosure to milch the buffaloes. This time he covered his mouth with veil. He carried with him the licking mixture for the cattle and the milching buckets. It was still dark. He spread his hand on the buffaloes back. They responded positively because they were accustomed to Tidda's hands. They were totally unmindful for the woman's dress.

Tidda put some water in the milching bucket to wash the teats to remove dirt. He took some water in his hand and sprinkled it. The buffalo turned its neck to look towards Tiddi. Yes, it was in Tiddi's dress. It cannot be other than Tiddi. But shower of water was bit harder. The Buffalo tolerated it. Another shower was harder than the first. The buffalo moved its hind legs to show some resentment. Tidda produced "*puch-puch*" or a fondling sound from his mouth. The buffalo raised its ears and became attentive. Tidda started mumbling the teats before milcking. It was a teasing experience for the buffalo. It struck the bucket with its legs. Bucket hit Tidda's knee. He was annoyed. He again tried to touch and press the teats for milching. But this harsh touch did not suit its teats. It moved onward, Tidda became angry and hit the buffalo with a hard staff. The buffalo uprooted the stub. It ran outside as the door of the enclosure was not bolted.

Tidda ran after the buffalo. He forgot that he was wearing woman's dress. The *odhni* or shawl slipped from his head but he was still wearing the *ghaghri*. Jhabdu potter's donkey went astray that night. He was out to search his animal. But instead of animal he saw half man and half woman. He thought it to be some "Nar-Nari-Avatar" or some God-Goddess. It ran after Nar-Nari-Avatar to know about its donkey because Gods-Goddesses are all powerful. He tried to touch Nar-Nari-Avatar's feet but Tidda kicked him with force. Though Tidda's kick was forceful like Jhabdu's donkey but he tolerated it for a better cause.

Jhabdu was young. He gripped Tiddas feet. Some other villagers also gathered there. They were surprised to see a Nar-Nari-Avatar in their village. They started raising slogans in praise of this God-Goddess. The shouting of the slogan was so high that Jhabdu's donkey began to bray. Jhabdu thought that it was due to the blessing of that Nar-Nari-Avtaar.

Darkness shrinked and it was day break. Tidda removed his ghaghri. People recognised him. Even his buffalo recognised him by his beard. It bellowed, he caught it by rope. He brought it back to in its enclosure. As Tidda was not allowed by the buffalo to milch, he thought it wise to free its calf. The calf enjoyed a bellyful milk party for the first time in his life.

❄ ❄ ❄

43. Mother's Debt—Unpaid

Every mother desires that her children—may be son or daughter, should be promising. She pins her hopes on him or her right from inception. There is a rich tradition of *Jachcha* songs in which songs about pre-born and recently born children are sung not only by the *Jachha* but by the women-folk. A rich folk literature full of *lori* or lullabies is available in sanskrit, and all standard languages. In lullabies mother wishes that her son should live a healthy-prosperous and long life. He should honour the healthy family traditions. Hari Singh Nalwa's mother also had the same expectations at the time of her son's birth.

Those were the days of Jehads or crusades and unprincipled rulers. Their main desire was to loot, kill or annex other ruler's territory. Some times the petty rulers of different religious formed a junta to win and divide the territory of a powerful ruler. The rulers bestowed big royalty, *jamin-jayadad* to their warriers. Even bards sing songs of their chivalrous and heroic battles. Hari Singh Nalwa is also sung in songs. His name was a symbol of terror especially among small children in Afganistan. When a child becomes out of control he or she is reminded of *Hauaa* or *Koka* as fear. *Havva* or *Koka* are supposed to be child killers, child eaters or child lifter.

In the early fourth decade of the nineteenth century Maharaja Ranjit Singh ruled over Punjab. With the help of his warriors like Hari Singh Nalwa he conquered Jammu-Kashmir. He wanted to teach a lesson to a *Jehadi* ruler in Afganistan. The fort of Peshawar was thought to be invincible. Hari Singh Nalwa crumbled it and as a punishment he mercilessly killed who so ever came in front of him including the infants.

Nalwa's happiness knew no bounds. He thought that he had kept the chivalrous tradition of his family. His mother would be happy to learn the victory and heroic deads of his son. He would pay all the debts of her mother by fulfilling her highest desire. In the most proud style he asked his army officers to march to his residence so that his mother could feel proud of his warrior son.

As per his command his followers followed Nalwa with great pomp and show like victorious soldiers.

He reached his village. He descended from his horse. The horse neighed. Nalwa's mother heard horse neigh. She supposed that his son must have returned safe after a great war and heroic expedition. She opened the door. Nalwa stood before her with extra—expanded chest. He informed her about his victory over the fort of Peshawar. He narrated that he has killed his bravest enemies. She should bless her son.

Nalwa's mother kissed his forehead and patted his back. Tears rolled down her eyes to see his wounded son. She recollected her husband and his chivalrous wars.

Nalwa said, "O mother, why tears in your eyes. I have won an invincible war. I have smashed and dashed my enemies. This is a day of joy and rejoicing. I will repay your debts. Just utter and I shall fulfil it. I want to be undebted from my mother's debt.

Nalwa's mother looked towards him most innocently. She smiled hearing the word 'repay of debt' from her son's mouth. Before Nalwa's return she was cleaning the floor of her room with a wet cloth. It was still in her hand. She spread the wet cloth on a bench and asked him to sit on the cloth till she return. She may bring glass of hot milk to offer him as a reward.

She spread the wet cloth and tried to go inside the house. In the mean time the heroic, chivalrous victorious and great warrior son lost his control and shouted, "O mother, this is the highest insult of a warrior. Why should I sit on this wet-dirty cloth? He deserves a *simghasan* or throne in its place."

Nalwa's mother smiled on her son's innocence and said, "Do you want to be indebted by giving worldly offers to you mother? I slept on wet beds for years to protect you from wetness and cold. You cannot sit over this cloth just for a while."

Nalwa felt ashamed. He knelt at her feet and sobbed for his arrogance.

❄ ❄ ❄

44. A Merchant and a Goldsmith

Once a merchant and a goldsmith lived together in a village. They were good neighbours. They helped each other in their day to day needs. Their children played together. They were very considerate for each other. But they never spared each other in their trade dealings.

Their firm belief was that trade is trade, money dealing is money dealing. Friendship should not interfere in dealings. If a horse develops friendship with grass it will die of hunger.

They had to travel together on various occasions. They kept their accounts separate. If a single paise was due to either of them they would account for it. This type of fair and clear dealing was the basis of their friendship.

Once they were going for trade. They had big *thailies* or purses made of cloth tied around their waists. Silver coin was the main currency in those days. When tossed a silver coin on thumb and forefinger and the pure coin produced jingling sound. The base coin mixed with *raanga* or pewter, tin etcetera will not produce any sound. People tested them by dropping on the pucca floor. They used to rub them on hand or cloth. When rubbed the base coin left a dark stain on the palm or the cloth. The ultimate judge or the assayer was the goldsmith.

As the merchant and goldsmith were travelling through paddy field they were spotted by the thieves. Both merchant and the goldsmith became apprehensive. They suspected that some unknown persons were following them. They tried to hide themselves in some safer place.

The goldsmith hid himself in a deep ditch. He spread some straws on him. There were thick bushes in the ditch due to rainy season. The goldsmith was very safe. He could not be located by the thieves only the merchant knew about his hiding place.

The merchant was not so prompt and cunning. He tried to hide himself but his red shawl deceived him. He was located by a thief. He tried to resist but he was over powered by them. They searched his suitcase but nothing was available except some clothes and edibles. They were disappointed. One of the thieves forced him for physical checking. They located something wrapped around his waist. O, it was a treasure. The sewed cloth *thailies* or purses were filled with systematically arranged coins. The merchant was helpless. To save himself from physical torture he handed over the *thailies* to the thieves.

The thieves tore open the silver and gold coins. They judged them to know whether they were base or pure. The merchant felt himself looted in all respects. But his co-traveller, the goldsmith was safe. The merchant was loser and the goldsmith was a gainer. He could not tolerate it.

He said to the thieves not to waste their energy in testing the coins. They can get them tested by a goldsmith. He can assure them that he never trades in base coins.

The thieves said that they did not want to take a risk of going to a goldsmith in some market. They would accept them in what ever form they were. If they go to a market he would get them arrested. They did not want to be trapped by his oily tongue.

The merchant thought that he had missed his mark. Goldsmith will remain safe. He again told them that they need not go to market. A goldsmith is hiding in a nearby ditch. He can guide them to that nearby ditch.

The thieves were over joyed. They followed the merchant upto that ditch. They located him and looted his money. Both merchant and goldsmith became penniless. The merchant was happy that their bargain finished on equal terms.

❄ ❄ ❄

45. Cunning Musaddi

Once there was a merchant. His name was Musaddi. He was very cunning and witty. One day he had to go on some business routine. He had four hundred rupees with him. On his way he had to cross a thick jungle. He saw four person coming towards him. They were thieves disguised as Sadhus. He felt himself trapped. He thought of a plan to evade them. He sat under a tree. He took out his purse and started counting money.

He bade good morning to them when they came nearer to him. They were surprised by his courteous behaviour. Musaddi said to them, "You have favoured me by your presence. I am a *dharmi-karmi* religious minded merchant. I donate four hundred rupees to four gentleman or Sadhus daily. I have to search out them with great difficulty. Today, I am fortunate that I met four gentlemen together. You have saved my energy and time." The thieves were happy to see such a gentleman.

But Musaddi said, "I have one difficulty. Please help me and solve it."

"What is your difficulty; tell us," said one of them.

Musaddi said, "I took bath on a nearby well. I had four *thailies* or purses containing hundred rupees each. I put them on the parapet of the well. I sprinkled sacred water on them to make them worthy of donating. Unfortunately two of them fell down in the well. Please help me in searching them out."

One of the Sadhus said, "We shall be satisfied by two hundred rupees. Donate us two hundred only."

"But what about my sacred *samkalpa* or vow. I have to justify it in my next birth. Please have pity on me", said Musaddi.

One of the Sadhus said, "Lead us to that well. I know diving. I shall search the purses out."

Musaddi led them to the well. The thieves tried one by one but would not get success as Musaddi's words were false.

Musaddi said, "Please take these two hundred rupees from me. Accompany me to my home. I shall donate the rest of the money at my home. My wife must be waiting for me. She takes meal only after serving me."

The thieves agreed. They accompanied him to his home. Musaddi's wife was surprised to see that four Sadhu's were accompanying her husband. She sensed that something was foul. A businessman can not return back before completing his assignment.

Musaddi said to his wife, "These are the four Sadhus to whom I wanted to donate four hundred rupees. As per Sadhu's temperament they live a lonely life in jungles. They have accompanied me here on my insistence. I had only two hundred rupees. I will arrange the remaining money. You prepare food for them."

Musaddi's wife provided the missing link of the story. She washed Sadhu's feet. She arranged best beddings for them. But did not waste money on cooking their food. The food to be served was totally different.

Musaddi went to the police station. He told police that the four looters have been entrapped by him. These looter have looted so many travellers so far. People were afraid of passing through that jungle.

Police inspector was happy on hearing this news. Accompanied by four policemen. He came to Musaddi's house with handcuffs in their hands. Street children saw the policemen. All the four 'Sadhus' were arrested (sooner or later they must have taken their meal in some jail). Musaddi was happy in his mission. No traveller was looted in that jungle thereafter.

❄ ❄ ❄

46. Chhailu, Chalti and Bhola

Once there were two brothers. One of them was Bhola Ram and the other was Chailu Ram. Bhola, as his name suggests, he was very innocent. He was a simple peasant who got up early in the morning and went out for working in the fields. He took with him plain and simple food and some time he had to chew and swallow the simple food with water. His dress was simple. He had only one pair of dress. It looked as if Bhola Ram was born to live this kind of simple life.

Chhailu, as his name suggest, was a dandy. He was a flamboyantly dressed person. As he ate rich food and took bath daily he looked very handsome. His handsome personality attracted his community. He was the Chaudhary or leader in the area. His main work was to while away his time smoking here and talking there. Always walking, talking, eating and drinking was his style of life. He would incite one party against the other and then settle the dispute as a cunning agent. Chhailu was liked by many and disliked by wise men.

One day Bhola Ram returned from the fields before midday. He saw that his brother Chhailu enjoying feast with his friends. He became jealous. He compared his hard life style with that of his brother. He threw his turban and announced, "O brother Chhailu, let us exchange our role or duty. You go for tilling, I shall do Chaudhrahat or leadership.

Chhailu smiled on Bholas innocence and said, "Leadership is not an easy job. It requires higher skill, manipulative power, farsightedness, trickery, deceitfulness, patience and other qualities like stone heartedness and what not. It is not a child's play. You will lose whatever you are getting. Do not try to become Chaubeji—six time higher in status—otherwise you will become *Dubeji*—half in your status.

Bhola resented, revolted and rejected Chhailu's advice. Chailu showed flexible behaviour like a good politician and offered him to exchange their duties forthwith.

Next Day Chhailu asked his brother to go to market and arrange for proper type of seed for the crop. Chhailu left for the fields. He enjoyed nature. It was a sort of picnic or a pastime for him.

Bhola went to the village market to purchase seed for the crop. Chalti, a lady was sitting on the seat of the seed shop. Bhola asked for seed. The lady charged the money and put his cloth inside the shop and said, "I shall supply seed only if you related me some *Urli—Parli* or strange and mysterious happenings of this or that side. Otherwise I shall not return you your money and cloth even."

Bhola was innocent in real sense. He had to cut a sorry figure. He returned home empty handed. He was a loser by all means. His brother had already warned him that leadership is not a child's play. Chhailu the brother returned in the evening. He was very fresh as he had passed a very lazy and free time after many days.

Bhola told Chhailu about Chalti, the cunning lady. Bhola felt sorry for his brother and asked him to exchange their role again. Firstly Chhailu resented just as a pretence. But the very next moment he accepted his brother's request.

Next day Chhailu went to the lady and asked her to supply the seed and return his brother's cloth. Chalti smiled as usual and asked him to relate some *Urli-Parli* or strange and mysterious happenings of this or that side. He came prepared to teach her a bitter lesson.

Per chance a *Sadhu Baba* came there and begged some flour. Chhailu said, "O *Sadhu Baba,* you can beg flour here any time. Someone is donating *Dhari* or five seer *laddoo* to everyone on the bank of the village pond near that temple." The Sadhu Baba at once ran towards that site. Chalti came with flour from inside her house to offer it to the *Sadhu Baba*. Chailu told her, "t the *Sadhu Baba* had gone to village pond where someone was donating *Dhari* or five seer *laddoo* to everyone. Keep this flour for him. He will return soon"

Chalti became impatient. She also ran towards the village pond to receive five-seer *laddoo*. Per chance the lady's husband returned after completing his work. He found a stranger sitting in the shop and his wife missing. When asked Chhailu told him, " a *Sadhu Baba* has eloped with his wife. You can catch them if you follow them without loss of time. They have run towards the village pond Temple."

The man ran swiftly towards the village pond. He saw that his wife was following a *Sadhu Baba*. Without asking her anything he gave her a good beating. She began to weep. He dragged her to his home. Due to severe pain she went on weeping. Chailu was happy because he conveyed to her *Urli* or this side of mystery.

The neighbouring ladies heard her lamentations. Chailu was standing outside the house. Now he decided to convey her the *Parly* or that side of mystery. He told the neighbouring ladies, " she is weeping inside because her brother is dead." Hearing this, all the women began to weep in her sympathy. It was a big fun for Chhailu.

Chalti came out from her house. She asked the neighbouring ladies the cause of their weeping. They put the same question to Chalti. She told her that her husband gave her a severe heating. She was weeping out of pain. Haven't their husbands beaten them also? The ladies saw each other's face. They said that they were told that your brother had died. Chalti asked the source of their information. They said that the man standing in front of your house broke this news to them. There was silence all around. Chhailu laughed and laughed.

Chalti became furious. Chhailu said, "You asked me to tell *Urli-Parly* story before giving seed to me. Now if you are satisfied, the story is over, give me the seed"

Chalti felt sorry and said, "You please take back your money as well as the seed and your cloth. I assure you that I shall never ask any customer to tell Urli-Parli story.

Chailu returned back to his home with full money, seed and the cloth. He told Bhola the whole story. Bhola was happy. Bhola Ram is still tilling the fields and Chhailu Ram is still the known Chaudhry or leader in that area.

❄ ❄ ❄

47. Karan and Vikram

Karan was a well known warrior as well as a famous donor. It is said that he used to donate *sawa-mana* or quarter and one mohnd of gold every morning. Time of sunrise is known as *Raja Karna's Samaya*. Karna was the son of sun god.

In those days there lived a king known as Vikram. He was very just and considerate. At night he disguised himself and personally noted the public grievances.

One night it began raining. He was far away from his home. He thought of staying at someone's residence. He took meal at a Brahman's house and paid five gold coins as a fee because he did not to take a free meal.

At night he slept at the doorstep. Per chance that was the *Chhathi* ceremony night in the house hold. A ceremony was being performed as it was the sixth day after the birth of a son. Women entering the house were crossing his cot. At midnight an old woman entered the house and she underpassed Vikram's cot. When she came out she again under passed his cot. He asked her who she was and why she under passed his cot. She said, "You are a *Kashatrya* and as a respect I under passed your cot. I know you. I am *Behmaata*, the divine mother. I write every one's fate on the sixth day. My words are indelible. They cannot be erased. They are inevitable. They are divine ordinance."

Vikram revealed his identity and asked the Brahmin to invite him to his son's marriage party. Time passed on. The Brahmin arranged his son's marriage and invited Raja Vikram. Raja came with his army. The Brahmin was frightened. Vikram told the bridegroom's father that according to *Behmata's* writing a tiger will attack his son. He has arranged a special box for the bride and bridegroom to protect them. Both of them will be encircled by elephants. The army will stand as strong guard. It will be a struggle between *Bhagya* or the fate and *Purushartha* or the human effort and endeavour. God blesses all.

When the marriage party was returning amid thick jungles the couple heard a roaring voice. The bridegroom wanted to know about the roar. The bride told that some tiger was roaring. The bride groom had never seen a tiger. He wanted to see it. But the box was very strong. They could not open it. The bride said that she can make a tiger's picture to show him. She rubbed out some dirt from her body. He too contribute his share of dirt from his body. The bride drew a tiger's picture from the dirt thus collected from their bodies. Fate was inevitable. The picture of tiger turned out to be a real one and broke the box after killing the bride groom.

Vikram was sorry for that unavoidable accident. He asked the marriage party to leave and assured them to make his personal efforts to bring the boy back to life. He asked his guards to smear the body of the boy with a special balm and to place it in the middle of a water pond. He ordered them to guard the dead body till he returned.

Vikram reached Raja Karan's court and offered his services to become his personal guard. Karan agreed to keep him his personal guard. Karan used to donate quarter and one mond of gold to the beggars. After two or three days Vikram noted that Karan left his cot very early in the morning and went outside and returned with gold. One night Vikram followed Karan stealthily.

Vikram saw that Karan jumped into a big frying pan. It was full of boiling oil. A *Sadhu* brought him to life and paid him quarter and one mond gold. Vikram returned home before Karan. Karan did not notice it.

Next day Vikram arranged a special anti burn balm to smear his body. He went to the same Sadhu in the dead of night. It was quite dark. Out rightly he jumped into the frying pan. The Sadhu took him out as was his daily routine. The Sadhu was very happy that day. He said, "I am highly pleased with you. Ask something special from me."

Vikram said, "I am well off by your blessings. I do not need anything."

When the Sadhu insisted him thrice he said, "You kindly give me three words or promises to be fulfilled."

The Sadhu promised to fulfill three desires. Vikram said, "As a first desire kindly give me *Amrit Ghat* or nectar casket. As a second desire give me *Gyan Gudri* or knowledge book. As third and final desire give me a moving wooden foot so that I may travel the entire world."

The Sadhu said, "I fulfil my first two promises. Do not ask for third. I will like to go somewhere else." Vikram agreed and returned with his prize.

After sometime Karan reached that spot. He saw the frying pan lying topsy-turvey. He was shocked to see the situation. He shouted for Sadhu Baba. Sadhu Baba said, "Why have you come for the second time? Are you not satisfied with the two precious things offered to you. Please go back and never come again."

Karan implored, "Sadhu Baba, are you in your senses? I have come for the first time. Please give me gold. The beggars must be waiting for me. They call me *Daan-Veer*, a big donor. I will lose my prestige and name."

The Sadhu expressed his inability. Karan returned empty handed. He was feeling highly dejected and rejected. He layed down on his cot. The beggar waited for him for some time. They started returning to their homes with great disappointment. Karan could not show his face outside. He decided to kill himself. Vikram felt pity on him.

Vikram said, "Call the beggars back. Donate them gold as per routine."

Karan said, "Someone has cheated the Sadhu. He went in my guise and begged everything from him. I got the gold stock daily from him after a great sacrifice. No one knows it. I am helpless. Let the beggars go back. I cannot face them. My name as a Daan-veer will disappear from today."

Vikram said, "I am Raja Vikram, your guard. I brought these articles from him. You need not go daily for sacrifice. Take this *Gyan-Gudri* from me. Produce as much gold as needed every day."

Vikram offered *Gyan-Gudri* to Karan. He returned with Amrit Ghat. He sprinkled some drops of nector on the body of Brahman's son. He immediately came to life. Vikram accompanied the boy to his home. Everybody was pleased. All praised Vikram's manliness, chivalry and bravery. He gave a befitting fight to fate. Karan is still known for his spirit as Daan-Veer.

❄ ❄ ❄

48. A Buffalo Owner

Once there was a farmer. He owned a big farmhouse. But his main profession was to sell buffalo-milk in the township. Many milk vendors assembled in the early morning for collecting milk. He was so skillful in cattle rearing that he could foretell about the milk yielding capacity of a she-buffalo at the time of its birth. If some buffalo withheld some milk in its udders out of affection for its young one he would immediately sense its mischief and give it a beating with a staff. The buffaloes used to sense his mood by his looks and movements. They would produced a flattering bellow to please their master.

The villagers called him Bhainswaala. He was very ambivalent in his temperament. In needy days he would revere Gods and Goddesses. He would arrange *Kheer* party on every *Amavas* or the full darkness night in the name of *Pitars* or paternal ancestors. He would sell only one fourth of the milk on that day. People thought that he was very religious. On certain occasions, he resorted to calling bad names to even Gods-Goddesses. He thought himself all powerful. In the heart of their hearts it so happened that villagers called him too selfish.

Once one of his milching buffalo strayed away to the fields after having dips in the village pond. Green grass and harvest attracted it. It moved on and on. Even its foot-prints became invisible. All the other buffaloes went to their proper stakes or tethering pegs as per their habit. One *Khunta* or stake was vacant. Kishnu, the Bhainswala's son, noticed it. *Rundhi*, as they called the buffalo, was the highest milching buffalo. This *murra* breed buffalo yielded twenty kilogram milk twice a day.

Kishnu immediately brought this big loss to his father's notice. Both of them took their strong staffs and went to the astrologer. They offered *Swa-rupya* or one and a quarter rupee on the astrologer's *Patra* or almanac and requested the astrologer to give some hint about their buffalo's where about. The astrologer after inquiring the time of loss told that it had not been stolen. It has gone to the South-West direction on its own. It may be located in some local pond with shallow water. The father and son felt satisfied with the astrologer's prudent guess and moved towards South-West, the forest side.

As Bhainswaala moved South-West he saw Hanuman's temple. He asked his son Kishnu to wait outside. He himself entered the temple and bowed before the image of Langota Hanuman. He said, "O Langota Human, if I get back my *Rundhi* buffalo I shall offer its one teat's milk i.e. one fourth of the produce to your temple daily". Bhainswaala again bowed before the idol and came out.

Both, father and the son, again marched on their search mission. On their way Bhainswaala noticed Lord Shiva's temple. Bhainswaala again asked his son to wait outside till he returns. This time Kishnu followed his father stealthily. Bhainswaala bowed before the idol and said, "O Jatadhari Shiva, my *Rundhi* buffalo has strayed away. I am on a mission to search it out. If I get it by your grace, I shall offer its one teat's milk to your temple daily." Kishnu heard his father's words. Bhainswaala again bowed before the idol and came out.

It was noon. Hot air was blowing. They were somewhat tired. They had their food packets wrapped in a cloth. They saw a temple. Both of them went there. Before taking their lunch Bhainswaala asked Kishnu to offer prayers in *Maata Kaali's Durbaar* also—Bhainswaala bowed before the idol and said, "O *Kaali Maata*, my *Rundhi* buffalo has strayed away. If I get it back I shall offer its third teat's milk to your temple daily. Please be kind to me."

Kishnu was disturbed. He thought it wasbetter to return. If his father donates three fourth of Rundhi's milk to the temples daily what is the benefit of having the buffalo. Its fodder costs them a lot. He would have to serve the buffalo daily. He would have to visit these far off temples daily to offer them their share of milk. But his father was all powerful in the family. He was also a mighty *Pahalwaan* or wrestler of his area. Kishnu did not register his protest and followed his father like the most faithful son.

As the sun was about to set they saw a greenery. It was Bhairo Baabaa's temple. Birds had returned to their nests. They were jumping from boughs to boughs and producing chirping sounds. Peacocks and Cuckoo birds were making shrill cries. It was a consoling environment. Bhainswaala sensed that he has reached his destination.

Bhainswaala entered Bhairo Baabaa's temple. Kishnu followed him. As his father was to bow before the idol for begging and praying he stopped him and said, "O merciless father, please do not beg and pray before this idol. What is the use even if we get our *Rundhi* buffalo back. You will offer its fourth teat's milk to this god. What will remain with us? I shall have to serve *Rundhi* daily just for nothing."

Bhainswaala did not heed his son's request. He was, if not *sachcha*, but a *pacca neta*." He had assured his followers several times at the time of voting and never fulfilled his assurances. He said to his son, "O Kishnu, let me pray for the last time. Do not come into my way. I shall see all these God-Goddesses if I get back my dear *Rundhi* again."

This time he prayed in his loudest voice. It was an open jungle. As he uttered the word *Rundhi*, the buffalo which was lying in the nearby shallow pond bellowed. It turned its ears towards the well known voice. It smelt the air. It noted its master's turban. It ran towards Bhainswaala and Kishnu. It began to lick Bhainswaala's staff just to please him and to be pardoned. Bhairo Baabaa, *Runndhi*, Bhainswaala and Kishnu were face to face. Whether Bhainswaala offered *Rundhi's* fourth teat's milk to Bhairo Baabaa is a matter of imagination.

He had changed his residence to some other, beneficial area. It is heard that he is still in possession of *Rundhi* and continuing in his milching profession.

❄ ❄ ❄

49. Amar Naam

Once a rich man lived in a township. He was blessed with a son by God's grace. He named him Amar. 'Amar' means immortal. Amar's father desired that his son will make his own name 'Amar' or immortal through his good deeds. When Amar grew up he came to know about his father's wish. He became interested in making his name unforgettable and immortal.

One day Amar was sitting idle on a common path. It was a sandy land. He was scratching the soil. An idea came to his mind for making his name known to everybody. He inscribed his name in bold letters on the sand. Many people passed through that way and read his name 'Amar'. He enjoyed the moments when people read his name. Amar spent his day till sun set. Fortunately or unfortunately a violent dust storm hit the area. His name inscribed on the sand was wiped away by the gushing winds. Amar was disappointed. He returned home in a gloomy mood as his name lasted only for some hours.

One day he was sitting under a big shady tree. It was on a busy cross road. Many people used to pass through that way. An idea came to his mind to make his name known to many people. He took out a knife from his pocket and inscribed his name 'Amar' on the trunk of the tree. He was happy to see his name in bold letters. Many people passed that way and read his name 'Amar'. He enjoyed the moments when people read his name. Amar spent his day till sun set. Fortunately or unfortunately a violent wind storm hit the area. The tree was uprooted. His name inscribed on the trunk of the tree disappeared as it was broken into pieces. Amar was disappointed. He returned home in a deep gloomy mood as his name lasted only for some hours.

One day he was sitting under the wall of a big old famous building. It was on a busy cross-road. Many visitors from far and wide used to visit that place. An idea came to his mind to make his name known to people from far off places. He inscribed his name stealthily on the wall although it was an act prohibited by law. He sat in a corner and enjoyed the moments when people from faraway places read his name. Amar spent his day till sun set. Fortunately or unfortunately a violent hail-storm struck the building. The building collapsed. His name disappeared under the debris. Amar was disappointed. He returned home in a dejected mood as his name lasted only for some hours.

Amar was planning to inscribe his name in some indelible way. According to him it could be through hammer and chisel on some stone. There was a mountain nearby. A rivulet flew under an attractive cave. Many tourists visited that venue every day. Amar went there with a hammer and chisel in the early morning. He engraved his name on a marble rock. Visitors, tourist parties from far flung places came there. Most of them read the name 'Amar' as it was engraved in bold letters on a prominent place. Some ascribed the word 'Amar' to the rivulet, some to the place of that site and some to the cave.

Once it was a rainy season. Black clouds overcast the sky. A torrential rain continued for a day and night. All the area was inundated. The rivulet was converted into a gushing river. The uncontrolled waves washed away even heavy rocks. When water receded Amar visited his pet rock. It was no more there. What to speak about his engraved name when the rock itself was missing. Amar returned his home with utmost dejection. He was failing in his mission time and again.

Incidentally a saint came to his township. Many householders visited him to get solution of their problems. The saint consoled them all. Amar also went to the saint and placed his problem before him. The saint suggested that the only way to make one's name immortal is to engrave one's name on people's hearts. Amar returned with saint's advice. He was over joyous.

Next morning Amar arranged an axe and a pen. With the axe he was to axe people and with the help of the pen he was to write his name upon the men's hearts. Amar saw a man going towards his fields. He ran after him. The man noticed a young man with an axe in hand coming towards him. He smelt some foul game. He became suspicious and ran back towards the village. Some villagers noticed them. They caught Amar by neck and asked about his motive for running after Bhola, the man.

Amar admitted frankly that he wanted to make his name immortal by engraving it on peoples' hearts as advised by the visiting saint and explained about the incident. The saint when he came to what had happened just smiled on Amar's extreme innocence. He explained the meanings of engraving one's name on people's hearts. It is only through immense service to humanity that one can find a secure place in people's hearts. It is possible through helping the poor, providing service to the needy and diseased and educating the needy families.

Amar felt sorry for his ignorance. He donated his whole property in the service of the society. A hospital and an educational institution stand in his fields. The place is known as Amar-Ashram. His name has found a permanent place in people's hearts.

❄ ❄ ❄

50. Chakra and Khapra

The story dates back to the times of great battle of Mahabharata. Kunti, the first wife of Pandu was prevented by a curse from having progeny. Pandu allowed her to make use of a mantra or charm she had acquired from the sage Durvasa by means of which she could have a son by any God she liked to invoke. She went across the Himalyas and invoked Dharma, Vayu and Indra and had from them Yudhishtra, Bhim and Arjuna as progenies respectively. She had other two sons Nakula and Sahdeva.

In those days Drupada ruled Paanchaal. He learnt the science of archery from Drona's father Bhardwaja. Drona was his school fellow. Drupada had a daughter named Draupdi. When she grew up her father wanted to marry her to a person who was well versed in the science of archery. He arranged a *svayamvara* ceremony—public choice of a bridegroom by the bride from among her assembled suitors for Draupdi. According to the condition, a fish was hung on a long pole. Its reflection fell in the pan below which was filled with oil. The winner shooter was to shoot the eye of the fish by an arrow, seeing its reflection in the oil.

Drona, the school fellow of Drupada, taught the science of archery to the Pandvas. Arjun among them was the master shooter. He shot the arrow in the eye of the fish as condition prescribed for the winner. Drupada married Draupdi with Arjuna.

When the Pandvas returned home they told their mother that they had made a great acquisition. Where upon the mother said, "Well, then my dear children, divide it among your selves." Draupadi's father Drupada resented this decision when he came to know about it. Draupdi, a haughty princess, was also annoyed. Kunti told them that her words could not be changed whatsoever may come. Woman's words are final in certain ceremonies in their area. So Draupdi became the common wife of the five brothers.

Draupdi's misfortune did not end here. It looked that the proud princess was born to bear endless miseries. But one day her bowl of tolerance was sure to burst.

Duryodhana, the eldest of the hundred sons of Dhritarashtra and Gandhari developed a deep hatred since his early years for his cousins, the Pandavas. He made every effort he could to ensure their destruction. When his father proposed to make Yudhisthira, heir apparent, he did not like the idea. Draupdi had to take shelter in *Varnavata* with her husbands. Duryodhana caused a palace to be built mostly of lac, resin and other combustible materials thereby hoping to see them all burnt destroyed when they would enter it. But the Pandavas were forewarned and they safely escaped.

Draupdi was to face a most humiliating situation thereafter. Yudhishatra performed the *Rajasuya* sacrifice with great pomp and splendour at Indraprastha. This further excited the anger and jealousy of Duryodhana. He induced his father to invite the Pandavas to Hastinapura to play the game of dice. In that gambling match Duryodhana, who was ably assisted by his maternal uncle Sakuni, won from Yudhisthra everything that he staked. The infatuated gambler staked himself, his brothers and even Draupdi. She objected to her being staked by a person who himself had been lost already but of no use.

Draupdi was in menstruation period but still she was dragged before the royal assembly. Duryodhana pulled her *sari* to make her naked. Lord Krishna blessed her with endless *sari*. Duryodhana patted his thigh and asked Draupdi to be seated on it. It was too much for her. She roared like a frowning Goddess. She vowed before the assembly that she would not tie her hair till they were soaked with the blood of Duryodhana's thigh. She taunted her husbands for the very same way in which they put up with the insults and injuries inflicted upon them by their enemies.

Draupdi was forced to go for exile with her husbands for twelve years and to pass an additional year incognito—*agyat vaasa*. On several occasions she saved her husbands when they were put to test. Once Durvasa begged food for his 60,000 pupils, she played a trick and saved their husbands from the rishis's curse.

During exile she had to act as a maid-servant or 'sairendhri' to Sudhenshna, the queen of *Virat*. When Kichak Sudheshna's brother tried to molest her she was saved by Bhima and Kichak was killed.

The fire of revenge always disturbed Draupdi. At last the great war Mahabharata broke out between the Kauravas and the Pandavas. Krishna acted as Arjuna's charioteer. Arjun raised his bow against several redoubtable warriors and vanquished them. On the 18th and last day of the war Bhim fought duel with Duryodhana and smashed his thigh with his club and Draupdi soaked her hair in that blood.

When the war was over Krishna drove Arjuna to Indraprashtha in the war-chariot. Arjuna became proud. When Krishna asked Arjuna to climb down the *Vijai Ratha* Arjuna refused. Why should he, when he had won the war single handed. Krishna smiled to and decided to break his false pride. He tried to convince him that some other unseen forces have killed the enemies. Arjun did not buzz. After great persuation Arjun jumped from the chariot and it was turned to ashes. Arjun did not realise the power of unseen forces which worked in the war.

Krishna accompanied Arjuna to a nearby *sisam* tree. A head without body was hanging on it. It was Barbareek's head.

Barbareek was a great warrior borne to Ghatotkach and Kamakantka. He wanted to see Mahabharata war till its end to know who sided with Dharma. Krishna begged his head guised as Brahman and beheaded him to save people from total destruction in war. He hung its head on the top of a tree. He blessed him with the power to see war. The head watched the entire war in a neutral way.

When asked about the forces who won the war the head said, "I have noticed two active forces responsible for winning the war. The first was '*Chakra*' borne by Lord Krishna and second the '*Khapra*', the skull bowel borne by Draupadi as Goddess *Khappardharni*".

Arjuna felt ashamed. His false pride was broken. He knelt at Krishna's feet and begged pardon for his false ego.

Lord Krishna was happy with Barbareek for his plain speaking. He blessed him by giving him his own name '*Shyam*'. In *Kaliyuga* people worship this great warrior as *Shyamji* and pray for his blessings. The famous temple of *Shyamji* of *Khatu-ka-Shyam* is situated in *Khatu* village of *Seekar* district, in Rajasthan. An annual function is held in this village on the twelfth day of the bright half of the lunar month, *Phalgun*, the twelfth month of the Indian Calendar.

❄ ❄ ❄

51. Yama Doot and Manmauji

Yama is the God of death. His seat is Yama Loka. He has countless messengers. They are known as Yamadoots or Yama's messengers. Through these messengers he keeps the records of human deeds. He visits Bhoo Loka or Mritu Loka once a year i.e. on Bhaiya Dooj—the second day of the bright half of lunar month, Kartika, the eighth month of Indian Calendar—to take meal with his sister Yamuna. His messengers, Yama Doots are very dutiful. They show mercy to none.

Once a Yama Doot was visiting the earth to records people's deeds—good or bad. He met a man Manmauji. The man knew the art of making friendship. He won hundreds of friends. He got his problems tackled through them. Manmauji was attracted towards Yama Doot due to his strange attire. When contacted Manmauji was shocked to know that he was shaking his hand of friendship with Yama Doot. He may immediately dragged him to Yama Loka. But Manmauji was a positive thinking young fellow. He counted plus points for developing friendship with him. Through the Yamadoot, he could postpone his death for a long time. Or at least he could inform him in advance so that he may manage his worldly affairs properly.

Manmauji conversed with Yama-Doot with an oily tongue. He praised Yama Doota's courage, valour, insight, righteousness and so many other good traits. Yama Doot was flattered by his praise. He shook his hand of friendship with Manmauji. Manmauji was happy that he had entrapped even the Yama Doot.

Manmauji and Yamadoot met off and on. One day Manmauji said, "Dear friend, can you spare me from death? I fear from it."

Yama Doot said, "No one in this earth is immortal. Their deeds are such. People cheat each other. They speak untruth. They even ignore God who has created them. Death is sure to everybody—sooner or later—We, the Yamadootas, are very sincere to our Lord Yama. Friendship cannot come in between our duty and sincerity."

"But still you must have some local powers, said Manmauji. "You can warn me before death so that I could manage my worldly affairs in advance. I may be mentally prepared to undertake that long-long journey. Please drop a letter in advance."

"But you cannot decipher my script," said Yama Doot.

"That is my duty. When I can understand peoples mood in advance, can I not decipher your message? Do not take me as a child. Your script will not be in poorly formed characters," said Manmauji boast fully.

Yama Doot said, "My message will be not in delibel ink. It will be indelible provided you have proper eyesight to see it and teeth and tongue to pronounce it. Please do not undermine or ignore my message. Do not try to pretend that you did not receive it. Yama Doot smiled on Manmauji's false pride and innocence.

Manmauji thanked his new friend for his assurance. He said, "I am a busy man. I am always overburdened with my professional work and homely affairs. If I do not respond, please send me one or two reminders. I am so busy day and night that I cannot spare time even for death."

Yama Doot said, "Yes, I give you words. I shall send three messages. If you ignore them I shall be forced by my master to take you away without wasting a single minute. Now permit me to leave because I have multiple responsibilities."

Yama Doot disappeared. Manmauji was highly delighted. Now he always had his own ways of life. He became an "eat, drink and be merry" type of person. Why should he worry? He would be cautious when he would get some letter from his friend, the Yamadoot.

Time passed on. He became half-aged. Day by day his hair became grey. His wife cut jokes with him. He consulted some vaidyji who recommended black henna to dye his hair. He was overjoyed to see his hair black. Now his wife too was happy because her husband did not look old. She looked a befitting match with him.

Time passed on. His teeth began to decay. His teeth began to fall one by one. His mouth became teethless. He went to some dentist. He fixed new teeth. He looked his face in the mirror and smiled. He looked young. His wife too was happy because her husband could chew hard food.

Time passed on, Manmauji's eye sight began to fail him. He failed to recognise his own children. Sometimes he tumbled because he could not see hurdles on the road. He went to an optician. He recommended eyesight glasses for him. Manmauji saw his face in the mirror. He smiled in it. His teeth were very bright. His hair looked black. He was a young man. His wife was happy because her husband could locate his articles for daily use himself.

Manmauji noted that most of his contemporary fellows looked old. Their hair was either turned grey or they became bald headed. Their mouths were shrunken due to missing teeth. They used walking stick to locate pits or hurdles. Most of them visited temples and religious gatherings for discourses. Some tell beads to perform devotions. Some of them visited holy places to seek blessings for long and healthy life. People from different religions and sects performed their rituals according to their beliefs. They were well prepared for their next birth's journeys.

Manmauji was quite unmindful about those worries. And why should he be when he had a special friendship with Yamadoot. His trusted friend, Yama Doot had not written even his first letter to him, not to speak of the reminders. He was still passing a happy go lucky style of life.

Once Manmauji suddenly fell ill. Some fatal illness overpowered him. He took best medicines but all in vain. He was bed ridden. He could not move his organs. He did not apply dyer on his hair. His artificial teeth were of no use because *vaidyaji* recommended him vegetable soup. They were set aside by his wife. His spectacles became hurdles while covering and uncovering him with quilt. His eyesight was very weak but still he could recognise when someone spoke to him. His tongue was failing him but still he could speak haltingly.

Suddenly Yama Doot appeared before him. He was equipped with Yama paasha and assisted by four assistants. He bore fiery looks. Manmauji recognised him with his facial expressions and way of talking. He said, "Why have you taken unwanted trouble to come here to deliver your first message to me. You could have sent your pretty messenger for this ordinary job. I feel sorry for it. I ask my family to entertain you because you have undertaken a long-long journey. Any way you have kept your word. Your message is well received by me. I shall read it when I recover from this deadly disease."

Yama Doot heard him patiently and said, "I have come to take you to Yamaraaj. Do not waste my time in indulging in tall talks.

"But what about your old word? Have you kept them? You claim to be the representative of Dharmaraaj and back from your assurance and words, "said Manmauji.

Yama Doot said, "I sent three letters to you. You might not have read or deciphered them."

"Three letters"

"Yes three letters"

"On wrong address"

"O no, on your very personal address"

"Then, where are those?"

"The bearer still bears them"

"I bear them?"

"Yes you. You seem to feign or you could not decipher them. I still see them well embodied in you."

"In me"

"Yes in you"

"Where? How?"

"My first letter rests on your gray hair. You tried to deface it by sprinkling black dye on it. Look through mirror"

"Oh is it so?"

"My second letter knocked down your teeth. You chewed it down by artificial teeth"

"O is it so?"

"My third letter was when your eyes began to fail you. You blurred its letters through artificial glasses. Do not blame me."

"Oh, Oh, Oh"

"Now I cannot spare you. My master's order is inviolable. They cannot be deferred."

Poor Manmauji felt meek before Yama Doot. He lamented for his ignorance. Soon his soul was borne away for an unknown destination.

❄ ❄ ❄

52. Harnandi

Bhateri was the seventh girl-child to her parents. As a custom and belief she got this name, which means 'enough'. The parents wish no more female-child. By this name God will hear parents' prayer and will bless them with a son next to her birth. But as God's wish the plague broke out in the area. Many young and old people were swept away in no time.

The main attack of this was on twelve villages known as *Baarha Bhaichara* or brotherly relationship of twelve villages. They belonged to the same *gotra*—sub-division of the same caste group. Intermarriage of boys and girls among them was prohibited as they consider each other as their brothers and sisters.

Bhateri was the only surviver in her family. People say the female child is saved, protected and grown up by nature itself as nature is female. Sex favours sex. Bhateri was brought up by a lady who was issueless. Nature blessed this woman Bhartoi and milk began to ooze from her breast. Bhateri sucked Bhartoi's breast for two years without knowing the tragedy faced by her family.

Bhateri became skilful in homely activities very soon as if nature showered blessings on her. She learnt the art of cleaning, cooking, sewing and other agricultural chores. She could milk the cows, cut fodder and churn milk for taking out butter. She attained marriageable age and the main concern of the foster family was her marriage to some suitable bridegroom.

The main hurdle in her marriage, apart from being an orphan, was that she was brotherless. A bride without brother looses charm. Who would send presents to her on *teej-festival* or on festival days? Who would send *chhuchhak* on an important ceremony observed after childbirth when the brides family sends *piliaa* yellow printed cotton shawl and other presents for the new-born baby. The foster-family may not bear that burden.

The *Bhaat* ceremony would be the biggest hurdle. In *Bhaat* ceremony a married woman goes to her parents to inform them about her child's marriage and offers them some rice and *gur* a lump of coarse sugar, as a token. Songs are sung in her honour. It is a big family meet and show time. In return the Bhaati's or the sister's brothers attend the marriage party. They offer presents and ornaments to their sister. They receive a very warm welcome through songs, sung in their praise.

Bhartoi arranged her daughter's marriage with a handicapped boy because no one was ready to accept a poor woman's daughter. She was not in a position to arrange dowry, a big social evil.

As the marriage date was nearing Bhateri became very sad. Her problem was whom to visit in her parental village. There was no nearest and dearest relative. Harnandi, a legendary woman, went to his father, who was alive at that time. He was a devotee to Lord Krishna. Lord Krishna showered *Bhaat* and saved Harnandi's honour. But Bhateri had lost all in the plague epidemic.

She restored courage. She decided to offer *Bhaat* ceremony to the holy *peepal* tree on the outskirts of her ancestral village. She had heard a story in her early age that Lord Krishna visits *peepal* tree on every Saturday. She was told, "he is accompanied by his wife Lakshmi who comes to meet her sister *Dridra*. I am penniless like *Dridra*. Lord Krishna went to perform *Bhaat* ceremony to Harnadi because she had no brother. I am like Harnadi. I shall claim Krishna as my brother. He has a number of means to send his representatives. More over Lakshmi is very generous lady. She may acquaint Lord Krishna with my helpless condition."

So Bhateri reached *peepal* tree at the outskirts of her village on Saturday. She worshipped it with *roli-tilaka*, had *parikrama* or went around it seven times. She tied a *kachha* thread around its trunk as if it was *peepal's* wrist. Some women from her ancestral and surrounding villages came to perform *pujaa* on that day. Some woman recognised Bhateri and asked about her family wellbeing's. She told them that she had come to *perform Bhaat ceremony*. As she has no brother or any other immediate relatives living in the village she is performing this ceremony under this *peepal* tree. She offered some *Kasar*—a sweet made of flour fried in *ghee*—and *gur* to them. A strange feeling pricked the women when they accepted and tasted the *Kasar-gur prasaad*. They realised her sufferings and thought of repaying the credit due to Bhateri.

Bhateri returned to her in-laws village by evening. In the heart of heart she felt consoled because she had done her duty. The woman from her ancestral and surrounding villages returned to their homes. They talked about the *Bhaat ceremony* performed by Bhateri. Who so ever heard it was stunned. People talked about this incident. This news reached the head *Sarpanch* of *Baarha Bhaichara*.

People fulfil our unfulfilled desire in dreams. Bhateri had a dream that night. She was standing on the door-steps of her house wearing a costly dress. She had a *chaumukha—deepak*, filled with *ghee* and wavering with four lighted wicks, placed in a *thaali*. His brother put a costly shawl on her head and also on wives of elder and younger brothers of her husband. A big gathering of young and old ladies were singing songs in praise of the *Bhaaties*. Some women and children were standing in the balconies of the houses across the street on the opposite side. There was joy all around. Her dream was broken when a cat jumped from the *bilangni*—a rod meant for hanging the clothes to catch a rat. Was it a bad or good omen, she could not guess.

On the other side *Baarha Biraadri Bhaichara* called a meeting. The head *Sarpanch* related the whole story to the gathering why and how Bhateri performed *Bhaat* ceremony under a *peeple* tree in a lonely jungle. Many eyes were wet with tears when they remembered their dead relatives—young and old. Their daughters and sisters must have attained the same age like Bhateri. They must be preparing and arranging their weddings. The very imagination was so heart rendering and touching.

All the speakers representing nearby villages expressed one feeling—Bhateri is like our own sister and daughter. We stand for *Bhaat ceremony.*

Women arranged clothes and men folk the required ornaments and other articles. This news reached Bhateri. She could not imagine whether it was a gift granted by *Peepal* tree, Lord Krishna and Lakshmi or by the spirit of Gods residing in the people's heart. When the *Bhaaties* reached her doorsteps her dream came true.

The people living in Bhateri's in-laws village were surprised to look that scene. They equated Bhateri with Harnandi and she is still known by this name.

❄ ❄ ❄

53. Suicidal Act

Once there lived an old lady. She had a son. Both of them spent a peaceful life. One day the old lady said to her son," You are now quite grown up. You have attained a marriageable age. I will marry you to some beautiful woman."

The boy said, "Dear Mother, both of us are leading a peaceful happy life. There is every possibility that third person may disturb our peace."

The mother did not agree with her son and insisted for his marriage. The boy agreed and got married. The newly wed wife did not see eye to eye with her mother-in-law. She wanted to get rid of her mother-in-law.

One day the wife of the son said to her husband," Your mother is an ill tempered lady. She has made a hell of my life. I do not want to see her any more. Let her be done away with."

The man tried to convince his wife but she was very adamant. In villages ladies make cow dung cakes for burning purpose. After they are dried they are heaped at a safe place and a covering of cow dung is laden on the heap to save it from rain. One day the wife carried away cow-dung cakes from the heap into a jungle and arranged a pyre for her mother-in-law. Some ladies noticed her movements. The young lady told them that she was to raise a new heap of cow dungs. She wants to dispose of old heap."

It was night. The young lady made all arrangements to dispose off her mother-in-law. Her mother-in-law was having a sound sleep. The young lady asked her husband's help to carry away his mother's cot to the jungle. The young man said, "Do not dig pit for others. My mother is not so bad as you paint her to be."

The young lady threatened to commit suicide if he did not help her in carrying out her plan. The young man yielded to her wife's wishes. He carried his mother's cot with the help of his wife. The young lady lit the pyre and returned home.

It was a rainy day. Fortunately, the pyre did not catch fire. The old lady came out of the pyre and lay beside the pyre. Some thieves came to that site. They saw the old lady's body and the pyre. They took it as a good omen and went to the village side to made a bountiful theft. As the fortune helped them they got two golden bricks from a richman's house.

When they returned to that very jungle, they noticed a ghost like image crawling near the pyre. They were badly frightened. They ran away from the deadly scene. The golden bricks fell from their bag. The old lady picked up the golden bricks and brought them home.

The young lady was surprised to see her mother-in-law in possession of golden bricks. She asked the old lady, "How did you get these precious golden bricks?"

The old lady said, "I went to heaven. There is all gold. As I was old I could carry only two bricks. You are a young lady. You can collect as many golden bricks as you can."

The young lady felt happy. She arranged her funeral pyre with her own hands in the jungle. She lay down in the pyre. The same thieves came to that side to search out same golden bricks. They noticed the pyre and the dead body on it. As a good gesture they lit the pyre. The young lady was burnt to askes. She never returned to trouble her mother-in-law again.

❄ ❄ ❄

54. Imperishable Donation

Pandavas fought the great battle of Mahabharta against *Kaurvas* and were victorious. Yudhisthra, the eldest brother became the king. He was highly religious minded. He used to perform various types of Yagya. His subjects became very prosperous. His treasure room were full of *gems, jewels, gold coins* etc. He was proud of his treasure.

Once he decided to perform a *Rajsuya Yagya,* a rite which is performed only by a universal monarch. He wanted to donate plenty of silver and gold at the time of Yagya. He fixed the *Aakha Teej* day for a special donation so that his donation could remain imperishable. Prince, princess, kings and queens decorated their seats according to their ranks. *Pandits, Purohits, Rishis* and *Munis* were seated on the carpet for worship. The birds were singing songs in praise to make the occasion immortal. Beggars were happy to receive plentiful offerings in the form of cash and kind Yudhisthra's court was well set with kingly decoration.

To the great surprise of that selective gathering a mongoose began to roll under the canopy where the *Rajsuya Yagya* was being performed. Every one noted its strange behaviour. The mongoose body gave a golden glitter. The remaining half was brown.

Yudhisthra inquired the *Rishi* about that uncommon mongoose. The *Rishis* said, "Better you yourself find out the reality from the mongoose.

Yudhisthra said, "O mongoose, tell me the reason of your visit. I can donate anything to you. I can get the remaining part of your body wrapped in to gold.

The mongoose said, "I do not need gold from you. If you have made your donations most humbly and in proudless manner, the remaining part of my body will automatically be changed into gold by rolling at this place. But I doubt the change. Entire amount of your donations is not equal to the three handful of parched gram flour donated by a hungry *Brahman* at the cost of his family to a beggar in draught period."

Yudhisthra got anxious and asked the mongoose to relate that story. The mongoose said, "Once there was a poor *Brahman*. It was a long draught period. The *Brahman* could not arrange meal for the members of his family. They were at the verge of death due to hunger.

The *Brahman* went to the fields. The harvest had already been cut. He gathered some grains from the gleanings of the field. He parched the grains and prepared three handful of *sattu* or parched flour from those grains.

Lord Dharma wanted the Brahman to put to test. He disguised himself as a poor *Brahman*. He knocked their door when the family was about to take their meal. Dharma said, "I am very hungry. I am at the verge of death. Will you please give me something to eat?"

The *Brahman* gave his share of meal. Dharma was not satisfied. He asked more to eat. The *Brahman* donated his wife's share. Dharma still wanted more. The *Brahman* donated the food share of his son's wife also. The *Brahman* fulfilled the duty towards guest at the cost of his family. All the members of the family died.

"I was seeing that *Atithi Yagya*. I rolled on that spot and collected some grains left by Dharma. Half of my body turned to gold. I visited many *Yagya* spot and rolled there. My remaining body did not turn to gold. I have come here with high expectations. I rolled on this spot for judging your sanctity for donation. I got nothing but disappointment.

King Yudhisthir, the son of Dharma felt ashamed. He decided to take fast on *Aakha Teej* and resolved for selfless donation. Later on Yudhisthir got eternal salvation.

❄ ❄ ❄

55. A Clever Jester

Once there was a jester. He never worked hard. He was a shirker. He always played new tricks with his employer. He was very witty. He always played with the words and framed his own meanings.

One day he was totally out of job. He was very hungry. But how could he manage his food?

He passed under the high walls of a landlords palace. He shouted loudly, "I am an honest man. I am in search of a job. I can undertake any job. No job is big or small for me. Work is a God's blessing. Is there a needy employer?My employer will be blessed by God."

The landlord was standing on his balcony. He heard the man's shouts the man repeated his appeal time and again. The land lord was highly impressed by his appeals.

The landlord said, "I am in need of a person. I need a man who could plough my farms. But you are well dressed. How can you plough. Only a rough and tough man can plough the land. I do not think you are accustomed to ploughing?"

The man said, "Do not conclude your judgement by my looks alone. All that glitters is not always misleading. I always stick to my words."

The landlord was happy. He said, "What will be your daily charges?"

The man said, "I do not work for money. I always accept only daily food."

"Only daily food,"said the landlord.

"Yes sir, only daily food," repeated the man."

'But is there any other condition? Reveal it frankly to avoid any conflict between us' said the landlord."

The man said, "My condition is very straight and simple."

"What is it'? "Said the landlord.

"I do not work after taking my dinner, that is my weakness, "said the man.

"I do not mind your habit. I accept your condition. You are my employee and I am your employer," said the landlord.

The man said, "Well sir, how far is your farm?"

The landlord said, "First take your meal and then go to the farm."

The man took his meal and said, "I have taken my breakfast, please tell me how far is your farm?"

The landlord said, "It is about three miles away."

"Three miles away", said the man." Who will take my meal to the farm. If I come back personally my work will suffer. I will take my lunch here and now."

The landlord was pleased with his sincerity of work. He asked his servant to arrange lunch for the man. The man enjoyed his lunch.

The landlord said, "Now you go to the farm and plough the land."

"Well sir, well sir," said the man. "I will go to the farm. But who will bring my dinner to the field. I do not want to waste my time in coming back for dinner. I will stay at the farm so that I could start my work in the early hours next day. Why do not you arrange my dinner here and now?"

The landlord was still impressed by his sincerity towards work. He ordered his servants to arrange dinner for his new employee.

The landlord said, "Why do not you go to the field? You have taken enough food. Do not shirk work.

The jester said, "You are very harsh and hard taskmaster. You cannot keep your words for a single day."

"What, what, what are you saying? Am I a hard and harsh task master! How have I broken my words, said the landlord.

The man said, "I told you that I do not work after my dinner. I have taken my dinner you cannot ask me to work after my dinner. I will take rest. I will leave your house after rest. I cannot work with you anymore."

The man left the landlords house in search of a next employer. He thought of a new plan for the next to befool him also.

❄ ❄ ❄

56. Ill Words Invite Trouble

Once Lord Shiva and Parvati were basking near a cliff on Mount Kailash. They were in a happy mood. Lord Shiva cut a joke. He called her "Shyama" (a black woman) How can a woman tolerate such insulting words from her husband. She was enraged. She could not control her emotions.

She said to Shiva,"Your mind and soul have been blackened by the poison which you bear in your throat. Your emotion for love has been dried up by the ash which you apply on your body from the cremation ground. The moon which you bear on your forehead has let loose her black scar on you. Who can believe the words having more than one tongue. You have borrowed tongues from the serpents which you bear around your neck. I leave your company. I will return only when I become gauri (fair complexion) or I shall die far away from you."

Exchange of harsh words between husband and wife are common. But this was too much. Shiva tried again and again to persuade her that he never meant that much. But when a king, child and a woman stick to their stubbornness there is no returning point.

Before leaving her home she instructed her adopted son Veerak to keep strict eye on Shiva's movement and behaviour. She asked him not to allow any woman entry in her absence.

On her way she met Kusuma, her mother's maid seervant, who was given to Parvati in her marriage to serve her. Suspicious as she was, she asked Kusuma to keep an eye on Shiva. She instructed Kusuma to convey to her if Shiva try to come in contact with any other woman. Kusuma saluted her in obedience and Parvati left for penance toward mount. She sat in *samadhi* a state of profound meditation to win blessing of Lord Brahama to attain fair complex on i.e. to become Gauri.

Once Lord Shiva killed the demon Andhkasura. His son Aadi was in search of taking revenge. He pleased Brahmha by his profound meditation. Brahmha bestowed a boon upon him. According to the boon no one can kill him until he changes his body into other form.

By hard boom he changed himself as serpent and entered through an open drain into Shivas palace. Veera and Kusuma could not notice his entry.

Soon he disguised himself as Parvati. He wore sharp resemblance containing tiger's claws to tear away Shiva into pieces. He approached Shiva when he was sitting on his sleeping bed. Shiva was pleased to see 'Parvati'. He gave warm welcome to disguised Parvati with open arms, Aadi was pleased, when Shiva embraced him. His body was unlike Parvati. His response towards Shiva, was uncommon. Immediately Shiva smelt a foul play. Shiva gazed at demon's body which did not bear the known sign which Parvati born on her body.

Aadi tried to kill Shiva. He forgot that he would be killed because he had transformed his body as a serpent and woman. Lord Shiva struggled with the demon and killed him.

During their scuffle Kusuma peeped through a window. She noticed a woman on Shiva's bed. She thought that it was her prime duty to convey this happening to Parvati. She chose 'Pawana', the wind, as a messanger. She related the whole story to Veerbhadra also. He felt sorry for not performing his duty faithfully.

When Parvati received the message conveyed by 'Pawana' she was enraged. She stood up from her seat and roared like a lion. A lion and Brahma stood before her, Brahma was pleased by her penance. He asked for a boon.

Parvati said, "Lord Shiva is proud of his fair complexion. He called me "Shyama", please give me a boon to become "Gauri", a fair complexion lady so that I can return to him with honours and grace.

Brahma blessed him by raising his hand. Her body was split into two. The black one, called "Kali" rode the lion and moved towards mount Vindhya to kill the demon Durga. The other one, Gauri, came back to lord Shiva.

On her way back she cursed Veerabhadra to become a "Shila"- a stone statue in due course. When she reached Shivas palace Veerabhadra did not permit her to go into the place. He could not recognise her because from 'Shyama' she was transformed to "Gauri".

She pleaded with Veerabhadra time and again. Veerabhadra said, "A woman disguised like you entered Shiva's palace. Later on it was revealed that he was Adhi, son of Andhakasur, Shiva's dead enemy. He came with intention to kill lord Shiva."

Parvati's hatred toward Shiva cooled down. She felt sorry for her curse given to Veerabhdra, her adodpted son. Meanwhile lord Shiva came out of his palace. The two gazed each other with surprise. Parvati felt sorry for her malice thought towards her husband. She felt ashamed for her bitter words. Lord Shiva embraced her and the couple had a happy life again.

❄ ❄ ❄

57. A Mortgaged Prince

Once there was a king. He was well-known for his donations. A rich man, who was king's next door neighbour, was very jealous of him. One day the richman's wife went to the queen and talked about the king's spendthrift nature. She poisoned the queen's ears and warned her about the serious consequences if the king did not amend his ways.

The king returned to his palace after hunting. The queen said to the king, "If you go on donating, our prince will be a sufferer. We will be bankrupt."

The king said, "Wealth multiplies if we donate to the deserving. Put for a happy and peaceful family life, I shall act as you like."

The king stopped donations. After sometimes, the king became very poor. He had to sell his palace and other property. He had hardly anything to meet both ends. The queen said to her husband, "We have nothing to eat. Our son is our only property. Why not to mortgage him? I have a sister. She is very rich. Go to her and mortgage the son to her for sixty rupees."

The king went to his sister-in-law and mortgaged his son for rupees sixty only. The king had a bath on his way back to home. Unfortunately, his money was swept away by the tides. He returned home empty handed. The king and the queen decided to leave their home and earn their livelihood somewhere else. They decided to live a life of a woodcutter.

The owner of the jungle had banned the cutting of green trees. People were allowed only to collect dry and broken woods. The wood cutters had a very tough life.

On the other hand the prince lived with his 'mausi' or mother's sister. She had three sons. She sent them out for trading. Before departure she asked her sister's son to purchase two pure pearls for her otherwise he would be punished for his failure.

The boys loaded their ships with merchandise and sailed back for their home. On his way back the prince recollected the warning about the pearls. He decided to go back. The prince reached an Island. He did not find real pearls. He decided to commit suicide out of frustration. A Sadhu appeared before him and inquired about his problem. He placed his difficulty before him.

The Sadhu said, "Do not be worried. A marriage party will pass from this place. The bridegroom is of blackish colour. They would accept you as a temporary bridegroom. The mother-in-law will ask you about your willingness for marriage. You compose a verse and ask for real pearls. She would offer you the same.

As per the forecast a marriage procession passed through that way. They saw the beautiful prince and convinced him to become a temporary bride-groom. The prince agreed.

The marriage ceremony was over. The prince was very hungry. He asked the bride for some food. The bride untied the knot of her marriage apron and gave dry rice to him. The prince told him the whole story. The bride said," I shall remain with you. My marriage ceremony has been solemnised with you only."

The bridegroom expressed his inability. He said, "I have been mortgaged by my parents for sixty rupees only. They are living a woodcutter's life in a jungle where cutting of green woods has been banned."

The prince left the bride and went on his way. The bride got up at night. She found the real bridegroom missing. She disguised herself as a Sadhu. People came to her from far and wide corners for astrological problem. Once a man told the Sadhu that he has come from a land where cutting of green woods have been banned. The Sadhu got a hint and reached that jungle. The king and queen, turned wood cutters, asked about their son's welfare.

The Sadhu said, "Your son is all well. He will meet you soon. If he visits you, inform me, I will live here in a small hut."

The wood-cutter said, "How can he return? I have mortgaged him for sixty rupees. I cannot cut green wood. I cannot earn sixty rupees."

The Sadhu said, "You come early in the morning. Uproot my iron pair of tongs from my hearth. You will get some sticks. Sell them in the market and free your son from the bondage."

The woodcutter found a golden bangle under the tongs. He took it to the bazaar. He sold it for sixty rupees. The woodcutter went to his sister-in-law. He was surprised to see that his son has grown up into a beautiful prince.

He brought back his son with him.

The son told his father about his marriage with a beautiful girl. His father said, "A Sadhu lives in a nearly hut. He is an astrologer. He can suggest some way to unite you both."

The father went to the Sadhu and informed him about the safe return of his son. The Sadhu smiled and said, "Better you marry him with some beautiful girl. The father said, "He told us that he was married to a beautiful girl under hard circumstances. He will not marry again. You suggest how both of them can be reunited. My son is feeling very uneasy."

The Sadhu closed his eyes, uttered some words and said, "Send your son tomorrow. He will meet his wife in my hut."

The father was overjoyed. The disguised "Sadhu" arranged the bride's dress over night. When the prince went to the hut the Sadhu said, "Your wife is under my protection. But how can you prove that she is your wife?"

The prince said, "When I was hungry she gave me yellow rice to eat. Some yellow rice are still tied in my turban's knot as a remembrance." The Sadhu was happy to test the boy's faithfulness.

The prince said, "But how the lady under your protection can claim that she is the same with whom I tied my sacred marriage knot?"

The Sadhu said, "The girl told him that she cut one corner of her husband's turban. You can match the colour and size of the piece as a test. She will appear before you with that piece of cloth."

The prince was satisfied. The "Sadhu" went inside the hut to send his bride. She dressed herself as a bride and appeared with the yellow piece of her husband's turban. The prince was surprised that the piece matched with the turban's corner. He untied the yellow rice pieces and showed them to his bride. Both embraced each other. The bridegroom was overjoyed to learn that the Sadhu was no one else but his bride herself.

❄ ❄ ❄

58. Pawan Weds Anjna

Once there was a Banar Des well surrounded by mountains. Its forests were watered by springs, rivers, rivulets and well-timed rain. Its residents enjoyed all the facilities because it was well protected by its ruler Mahendra. God blessed king Mahendra with a beautiful daughter. He named her Anjna who later on gave birth to Hanuman.

Vidyadhar, the able son of Prahlad ruled in a nearly state. God blessed Vidyadhar with a handsome son. He named him Pawan. He grew up a great warrior who could face hundreds of soldiers alone.

King Mahendra wanted to give his daughter, Anjana, to a desiring young man. He issued the photograph of his daughter to far and near places. Many princes responded his call and sent their photos to king Mahendra. The king sent Anjana's photo to king Vidyadhar. He dispatched Pawan's photo through a special messenger.

Anjna saw Pawans' photo along with her friends and elderly women. All agreed that Pawan was a matching aspirant for her. Pawan was attracted towards Anjna and wanted to see her personally. But how was it possible? The customs would not permit him.

Pawan accompanied by his minister left to see Anjna stealthily. They stayed in Mahendras Capital for three days but could not have Anjna's glimpse. They mustered courage as they were disguised and went to Mahendra palace. When they were passing under a window they heard some girls chatting and talking about Pawan's photo. One of Anjna's friend commented out of fun that Pawan's photo was like salty oceans water. Anjna's photo looked like nectar. Pawan's heart was badly hurt by that derogatory comment. But Pawan's father had already sent an acceptance letter to king Mahendra for the marriage. Pawan was helpless.

Pawan agreed to marry Anjana according to the elder's agreement. He decided to teach her a lesson for that killing comment. When they got married Anjna's Paalki or palanquins bearers dropped her in Duhaag Mahal or widowhood Palace as per Pawan's order. She never knew it.

When Pawan did not visit her by late night she felt humiliated. She asked Basantmaala, the attendant girl, the reason for Pawan's absence. She said that he must be busy in some important royal work. When Pawan did not oblige her even the next night she was worried. Basantmaala revealed the mystery that she had to live now in her palace. Anjna fainted but her Baandi or attendant, arranged water for her and tried to console when she came to senses.

Meanwhile Raavana the king of Lanka, sent a letter to Vidyadhar. He said that he wanted to challenge, Pawan the youth who had married Anjana. Pawanalongwith 500 soldiers left for war. Both the forces faced each other for a long period without any decision.

One night Pawan felt restless. He was strolling on the bank of river Kareena. He heard a strange weeping cry. He was stunned. He asked his minister about that incidence.

The Minister said, "Here lives a loving Chakwa or a sheldrabe couple. They get separated at night. The female is crying for its male mate because she is all alone in this moonlit sweet night. Females are the most sufferers when alone.

Hearing his minister's sympathetic words for female, a strange stimulating feeling tortured his heart. He remembered his wife Anjana. He realised his duty towards her.

He talked to his minister. The minister unhesitatingly said, "You are a sinner. You leave the war field immediately and oblige your wife this night. I will face the enemy in your absence."

Pawan dashed to Anjna Her attendant sounded Anjana. Anjana said, "Please do not taunt. A day will soon come when we shall meet. He will realise his mistake." When Anjna heard sound of foot-steps on the stairs, she became cautious and shivered.

When they met, Anjna fell on her husband's feet and said why you gave me this Duhaag hood punishment of separation from the husband? Why you stayed away from me for twelve long years? Is it not a sin?

Pawan said, "Why you called me a salty oceans water and yourself as nectar? Was it not insulting and humiliation for me?"

Anjna said," Overhearing lady's conversation is a sinful act. It was our private life. It was my friend who used thosee words for you just out of joke. You are badly mistaken if you owe that comment to me. An Indian woman can never use any unbecoming words against her husband."

Pawan felt sorry for his misunderstanding. He called himself a sinner. Anjana welcomed Pawan with open arms. He spent five nights with Anjana and begged her permission to join the war front again.

Anjna requested Pawan to visit his mother's palace as a proof of his visit. She repeated that her mother-in-law was very suspicious. As Pawan had no time to spare he offered her his personal ring as a token and left for war.

After two three months Anjna's pregnancy became apparent. Female attendants of the palace talked about it and the news of her pregnancy was broken before Anjna's mother-in-law. She became furious. She would not listen anything about the ring as a proof of her son's visit. She disrobed her of rich dress and ornaments and gave her black robe to wear.

Anjna left for her parental home with Bansantmaala in those hours of distress. Her mother-in-law sent special messenger to king Mahendra to ban her entry, as she was an adulterous woman. When Anjna reached Banar Des her mother disallowed her entry. She was shocked.

It was a rainy season. Sky was over cast with thick black clouds. Thunder and lightening were heart breaking. Anjna was weeping bitterly. The path was dark. She could not notice a deserted Jhera or dry deep well. Both of them fell in it. It was dead dark night.

A strong thunderstorm swept the area. Trees were uprooted. An old tree standing on the bank of the well was also uprooted. It tilted towards the well and fell into it. Both the ladies were frightened. They fainted but when they came to senses they caught trees branches and came out side safely.

Not far from the well they met an old Sadhu whose white beard touched the earth. He felt pity on them and gave shelter in his cottage. They related their sad tale. The Sadhu consoled them. He said that bad days are always followed by happy days as light follows darkness.

It was the eighth day of the bright half of the lunar month Chaitra of Indian calendar. Anjna gave birth to a beautiful and healthy boy.

The Sadhu named him Mahavir due to his muscular body. After two days, Ketmi, Anjnas' maternal uncle was flying with his wife in his udankhtola or flying saucer, over that area. They noticed a cottage and glided down.

They were surprised to see Anjana with a small child in her lap. Anjna wept bitterly. Both his maternal uncle and aunt consoled her. All of them were sealed in that udankhotla. Baby Mahavir jumped from one lap to another out of joy and finally jumped out of that saucer. The bone of his Hanu or chin was tilted. His maternal uncle named him Hanuman. His maternal aunt called him Bajrang Bali due to his sturdy build up.

On the other hand Pawan returned home after winning the war. He found Anjna missing in her palace. Pawan's mother told his son that as Anjna was a pregnant by meeting with some outsider she ousted her from the palace. As Pawan knew the reality he dashed to King Mahendra, his father-in-law. Pawan was told that as she was not allowed to enter that palace she went to some unknown jungle with Basantmaala. Weeping bitterly and cursing his fate Pawan left for the jungle. He noticed the same deserted well where Anjna spent a night. When he peeped down he noticed a bright object at its bottom. He climbed down and picked up the bright object, it was his own ring.

Hope brightened his eyes because he was following the right path. But next moment he thought that she might had been eaten by some wild animal or had died otherwise.

When Pawan did not return for some days 500 soldiers divided in small troops, went to search him out. They reached the same deserted well. They were shocked to see that Pawan had arranged his pyre by collecting sticks and logs. He was about to set it on fire. The soldiers informed him that Anjna was safe and sound in her maternal uncles' home. Anjna's maternal uncle kept her and her father Mahendra also reached that place. All of them were happy to meet together.

Pawan took Anjna and his young son Hanuman to his home. They lived a happy life. The story teller says, "Let happiness come to one and all as he visited King Vdhyadhars' and King Mahendras' family."

❄ ❄ ❄

59. Repaying in One's Own Coin

Once there was a rich agent. He had direct dealings with a merchant in Delhi. His wife was very homely. She gave birth to a son. Later on he helped his father. He got married in a rich business family. Their income got doubled.

With the death of the rich agent, misfortune hovered over their family. They faced difficulty in making their both ends meet. His son Mangli had not much experience in business dealings.

One day Mangli's mother asked him to go to Delhi and seek help from the merchant because he was benevolent and religious minded. As Mangli was poorly dressed, he was turned away by the gate keepers. The merchant noticed it from the window and he was called back.

Mangli related his sad tale and requested for monetary help. He paid him four hundred rupees. He returned home happily. He spent one hundred rupees for food and clothings. His mother asked him to go to Calcutta and invest the remaining money in some business.

Mangli reached Calcutta. He saw some divers on the seashore. They charged rupees one hundred for each dive. They would dive and hand over to the bidder whatever they got at the bottom. There could be hollow shells or precious pearls depending on bidder's fate. Mangli took them as cheats but business is business. He tried his luck twice and got hollow shells. He had still a hundred rupee note. As a good speculator he tried his luck for the third time and got three precious pearls. Each costed three-lacs. Mangli became Naulakhiya. He decided to return home.

The diver warned him about cheats. He set the pearls in his thigh and balmed it. He supplied some extra balm for applying at home. He asked Mangli to join a party, which was returning towards Delhi. As departing advice he said," Go to bed when all the fellows have slept and get up before all. Some cheats may follow you."

Mangli thanked the diver and joined the party. A cheat also joined them. He suspected that Mangli had some precious stones. All the fellow travellers went to sleep. He feigned as if he was sleeping. The cheat searched the belongings of all. When he came near Mangali he shouted," Please get up. It is time to depart" The fellow travellers got up. The cheat was disappointed.

He sold Mangli to another cheat for rupees one hundred. The second cheat joined the party but he met the same fate. He handed over Mangli to the third cheat but the divers warning and friendly advice helped him.

Finally the third party handed him over to a very rich cheater. He asked the entire party to stay at his residence as honorable guests.

This cheater plotted a strange plan to entrap Mangli. He asked his elder daughter to claim Mangli as her husband. When the party was about to depart the cheat called police and informed that Mangli is his daughter's husband, is deserting her and going with this party. Mangli claimed that he is already married and the cheat had some ulterior motive. The police sided the cheat and Mangli was detained.

When night fell the cheat sent his younger daughter upstairs to snatch the travellers possessions by hook or by crook. She went to Mangli with a drawn dagger and threatened to kill him if he did not deliver his possessions to her. Mangli said, "You will feel sorry after killing me like that Banjara or trader who killed his faithful dog without knowing his worth" When she tried to know that story he related it with such details that the day broke out and she came down to her father unsuccessfully.

Next night he sent his younger daughter 'Satara' for the same purpose. Mangli said," You will feel sorry after killing me like that king who killed the baaz bird which saved his life." When she wanted to know that story, he related it in full details how the birds swept away the poisonous bowl from the king's hand which he took as pure water. After hearing the sad story Satara fell in love with Mangli and insisted on accompanying him. Mangli resented but she suggested him a simple way out.

The cheat's younger daughter Satara said, "My father has two camels. One can run for fifty miles a day and another for one hundred miles. I shall mark the hump of the camel which can run for hundred miles. Both of us will run away by saddling that camel at night. Mangli agreed.

When Satara came down she said, "Father, your plan will be successful tonight. Please spare some time." Her father was happy.

Next night both of them rode away on that camel. But Satara realised that she had saddled the wrong camel. When the cheat heard one camel bubbling he became suspicious. He found that Satara, his younger daughter, was missing. He saddled the camel and followed the footprints of the former camel.

Satara's camel stopped under a tree and did not move further. She saw her father coming towards them. Satara said, "O dear Mangli, do not lose heart. You please climb the tree. I shall follow you. You follow my instructions." Both of them climbed up the tree.

When Satara's father came under the tree she shouted, "O father, save me from his clutches. Please climb the tree."

Satara's father left the camel under the tree. When he was climbing up she asked Mangli to jump over the camel's saddle. Both of them settled in the suddle and kicked the animal. The cheat was helpless as that camel had no capacity to move on.

As Mangli was a married youth Satara said, "I shall not go to your house. I shall stay in a nearly Dharamshala. Visit me for any help."

When Mangli informed his mother about his earnings she was overjoyed. He took out the pearls and put balm on his thigh. The news of his earnings spread in the town. Mangli handed over the pearls to his mother. She placed them in her safe custody.

Kasturi, a woman cheat, lived in a nearby street. She came to know about three precious pearls. She arranged three artificial pearls and went to Mangli's mother. She showed her the pearls. Kasturi replaced the artificial pearls and slipped away with the originals.

Mangli returned from the city where he had arranged a bargain to sell off the pearls. He asked his mother to hand over them to him. When Mangli saw the duplicate pearls he fainted on the spot. Satara, disguised as a Vaidya, passed near Mangli's home and offered his services for proper treatment. When Satara touched Mangli with her soft hands he came to senses. The Vaidya said to his mother "Did anyone visit home to see the pearls?" Mangli's mother told her about Kasturi's visit. The Vaidya said, "Do not worry. You will get back your original pearls within a week." Tell me where Kasturi lives. The old mother said, "No one can look towards her house. She would take out the eyes. No one can raise finger towards her house. She would cut the finger." Satara said, "You take a pebble in your hand. Drop it near her door. The old lady agreed.

Satara searched out the whereabouts of Kasturis family. She disguised herself as an astrologer and peeped inside Kasturi's window. Kasturi noticed it. The astrologer said, "I am thirsty. I want to take water. Will you please oblige me." Kasturi was highly impressed by the astrologer's polite tone and called him inside. She offered him best seat to sit. Her house was full of cheated belongings. The astrologer said, "You are a rich lady. God had blessed you with seven sons. But you look worried? May I help you in solving your problem with my astrological knowledge?

Kasturi said, "I have seven beautiful sons. All are unmarried. No one comes forward to offer their daughters to them."

The astrologer said, "Tonight a lady will visit your home in the form of Lakshmi, the goddess of wealth. Arrange a platform for her. Light a earthen lamp. Place your most valuable articles before it, keep your door open. Ask your sons to stay away from home as she is shy by nature. She will bring the bride of your son this week."

Kasturi was empowered by the astrologer's actions. She did as advised. At midnight a women entered her house. She entered the door, collected the pearls and other costly articles. She broke open a part of the roof and disappeared. Mangli got back his pearls and thanked Satara for her courage and wisdom.

Next morning when Kasturi opened the room she found everything missing and a part of the roof broken.

Satara sought Mangli's permission for departure to her father's house. Mangli said, "How will your father allow you to enter there?"

Satara said, "This is not a problem. I shall arrange it myself, "Remember me again in needy hours."

Satara departed and Mangli lived a happy life for many years.

❄ ❄ ❄

60. Haryali Teej

It was the third day of bright half of the Lunar month, Shravan. People in rural area call it Teej or Haryali Teej. Teej festival was being celebrated all around. Idols of Krishna and Radha were being swung in the temples. Swinging ropes were set on the strong branches of the trees. Young girls and women were enjoying swinging in the gardens. Ladies were singing chorus Teej or Sharavan songs while swinging. They were in their best dresses. Ladies had applied henna on their palms and feet. Children were proud of their dyed palms with henna. Without caring for black thundering clouds and drizzles everybody was in full spirits. Green fields, tossing with tiny Jawaar-Baajra saplings were adding more charms to the festival.

All the members of the families enjoyed homemade sweets like—Purées, Gulgulas. At night all the children of Sanvalia's family sat around their grandmother to listen stories. Parvati, the dearest granddaughter said, "Daadi-Amma, why do we celebrate Teej festival? Why girls and women are especially in the best dresses and high spirit? Is it a women's day? Is there some story related to it?"

Daadi Amma was happy to listen to Parvati's volley of questions. She said, "Yes, a very interesting story is connected with this festival. It was a victory day of Parvati's love. All girls and women join Parvati in her love's victory.

Parvati felt shy when she heard her name connected with that story of love. Daadi Amma said, "Do not feel shy. That Parvati was the daughter of Parvatraj and Maina. This story dates back to thousands years back."

"Is it so?" exclaimed all the children. Daadi Amma said, "Listen to me attentively."

In good old days, Maina gave birth to a beautiful girl. She named her Parvati. As she grew up her parents were in search of a suitable match for her. One day as Maina and Paravatraj were talking about their daughter's marriage. Narad Muni appeared before them. Narad wanted to know the cause of their worry.

Narad smiled and proposed Lord Vishnu for Parvati. He revealed that the proposed bridegroom had agreed to their proposal. The parents were happy. When Parvati heard this news she was badly shaken. As a good faithful wife she always wished to marry only Shivji in all her previous births. Narad disappeared from the scene. Parvati fainted and fell on the ground.

Parvati's friends attended her. When she came to senses she told about her misery. It was a bolt from the blue to marry Lord Vishnu. She desired for Shivji and Shivji alone.

Parvati's friends suggested that she should pray for Shivji. He is very benevolent. He can be pleased. She should make up her mind for penance and fasting. But it was not possible at home.

Her friends said, "We shall arrange a drama for kidnapping you to jungles. You accompany us to some cave on the bank of some river. You sit for penance and fast for pleasing Lord Shivji. He will definitely bless you."

Parvati left for Jungles along the River Ganges in the Himalayas. Parvati collected some sand and erected Shivalinga. She sat in front of it. She ate nothing for many days and prayed for Shiva, day and night.

By the power gained by Parvati through her penance and fasting Lord Shiva felt a strange sensation in his heart. He realised that someone was in trouble and calling him for help. He stood up from his seat as it was shaken through the heart waves sent by Parvati.

Parvati's heart waves attracted Lord Shiva like a magnetic. He came straightforward to the cave where Parvati was undergoing a strong penance.

Parvati recognized sound of Lord Shiva's feet. She opened her eyes and touched his solemn feet.

Lord Shiva said, "Who are you? Why are you undergoing this penance and fasting? I am pleased by your prayers. You can ask for some boon. I shall grant you the same."

Parvati again bowed before Lord Shiva and said," I am Parvati, the daughter of Parvatraj and Maina. My parents want to marry me to Lord Vishnu as per Narad's proposal. I have always chosen you as my husband in all my previous births. Please accept me as your wife in this birth also."

When Lord Shiva heard Narada's name as middleman for marriage he smiled and said, I give you my words for marriage. But your parent's consent is quite necessary. Let us return to your parents."

Parvati's friends were delighted to hear Lord Shiva's consent. They started to sing praise songs.

On the other hand Parvatraj was worried when he saw his daughter missing. He thought that she must have strayed away from the path. She must have been eaten by some wild animal. He fainted and fell on the ground. His wife Maina consoled her husband and said, "My heart believes that she is alive and safe. She must be praying somewhere to fulfil her desire. Only a woman can know a woman's inner heart and desire. She must be annoyed by our proposal to marry her with Lord Vishnu. Please give me word that you will fulfill Parvatis' wish."

Parvatraj gained confidence by Maina's advice. He gave his word to marry Parvati with the man of her choice.

King Parvatraj sent his soldiers in all the directions to search out Parvati. Accompanied by only trust worthy soldiers he too left his palace with full resolve to find out his daughter. When passing near a cave Parvatraj heard women's voice singing sweet songs. He was surprised. He could not believe his ears. Who could be there? He moved towards that cave. He had a sign of relief when he saw Parvati among her friends there. Lord Shiva was standing in a blissful posture and mood. All the girls were performing the ceremony of Aarti with earthen lamps in their hands.

When the Aarti ceremony was over Parvati saw her father standing in front of the cave. She ran towards him. He embraced her with full love and affection-. He connected all the missing threads of the story. He recollected Narad's misleading smile. Lord Shiva and Parvatraj paid due regards to each other. Parvatraj requested Lord Shiva to accompany him to his palace for Maina's satisfaction.

All of them reached Parvatraj palace. The entire area was overjoyed when the news of Parvati's proposed marriage with Lord Shiva was broken by the royal pandits. It was a victory of real love.

All the women and especially girls jumped with joy. They applied henna and wore best dresses. They swung on swing ropes to express their happiness. They enjoyed best sweets. As a good gesture that day was named Haryali Teej and that became a regular annual festival. In some areas this day is celebrated in a month later i.e. in Bhaadon, the sixth month of lunar year.

❄ ❄ ❄

61. Ranga and Ranghar

Once there lived a goldsmith. He used to mix raang or tin in silver. He was nick named Ranga. He used to cast duplicate silver sword mixed with tin. No one purchased his products. His wife became angry with him. Ranga decided to sell off his products to some far off places. One day he set out on his mission.

In some other area lived a Ranghar. He was ill famed for selling adulterated ghee and milk. Once he filled a tin with cow dung and covered it with pure ghee. He set out for selling his product.

Ranga and Ranghar met in a local market. They exchanged their products at a very low rate. Both were happy and returned their homes.

Ranga's wife melted the ghee and it got mixed with cow dung. Both husband and wife scolded each other. Ranghar tried his silver sword on an object and it was twisted. Both husband and wife scolded each other.

Ranghar thought that the gold smith proved more than a match for him. Why not to befriend him for cheating adventures. Ranghar searched him out. Ranga gave him a warm welcome. Ranga served him dinner in a costly golden plate. Ranghar planned to steal away the plate. Ranga suspected him.

Ranga filled the golden plate with water and placed it on a chhinkaa or straw basket hanging on his coat. He was sure that if Ranghar would try to take away the plate water would spil on his coat and Ranga would catch red handed. Both of them indulged in tall talks. Ranghar thought it proper to snore as a pretext for sleep. Ranga called him to judge his sleep. He did not react. Ranga had a sound sleep.

After some time Ranghar got up. He stealthily and silently filled the plate with ask from the hearth. He picked up the plate and hid it in the mud of a nearby pond. He did not think it proper to leave his house that night. He returned and had a sound sleep.

Ranga was quite suspicious. He got up and noticed that Ranghar's feet bore scum and moss signs. He concluded that the missing golden plate had been placed in the stagnant water pond. He rushed to the pond and searched out the plate.

Ranghar took his breakfast and begged his friend's permission for his next mission. He thought the delay can spoil his game. The cattle may break the plate while drinking water from the pond.

Ranga wanted to embarrass him. He requested him to stay for one more night. Ranghar agreed. Ranga again served him dinner in the golden plate. Ranghar became curious and said, "How many golden plates do you have?" Ranga said, I have only one golden plate. I am serving you in the same golden plate today also."

Ranghar said, "I stole away this plate." Ranga said, "I brought it back." Both of them exchanged each other's tricks and had a hearty laugh.

Ranghar said, "Let us exchange our turbans and become fast friends. We can loot the world and can amass countless money." Ranga agreed and they proceeded on their mission. Chips of the same bloc came together. It was to be seen whether they would flock together.

They had hardly crossed twenty miles when they saw a big crowed mourning the death of a multimillionaire. By sun set the mourners paid their tributes and left his house. Ranga and Ranghar still stayed there. Dhanpat, the multimillionaire's son, thanked both of them and asked to return to their homes. Ranghar said, "Your father has ruined us. He borrowed a huge amount of money some years back and did not return a single pie. Even the interest money runs into thousands. Dhanpat assured them to check the records and pay back the amount.

Dhanpat asked his Munims to check the balance sheets but there was no trace. Dhanpat did not oblige them. Ranghar said, "We can call back your father's spirit. If the spirit admits will you pay back our dues?" Dhanpat agreed. They begged three days time to call back his father's spirit.

Both of them dig a tunnel under the multimillionaire's burning sight. Ranga entered the tunnel at night and spread straws on its opening. Big crowd gathered at that site.

When asked by Ramghar, Dhanpat shouted "O Dear father did you ever borrow a huge amount of money from Ranga and Ranghar?" A sound below the pyre sight resounded, "Yes dear son. If they happen to return, repay them a mule loading with silver coins." Hearing was believing. All of them left the sight, Dhanpat arranged the money.

Ranghar said to himself, "Why not to enjoy the entire money myself? Why not to close the opening of the tunnel? Let Ranga converse with the multimillioner for years to come."

The nasty partner shut the opening of the tunnel and collected the mule loaded silver coins from Dhanpat next day. Ranga came out from the tunnel as the earth was still fresh and he was skillful in the art of digging.

Ranga hid himself on a tree near the main path of the city. He noted Ranghar's movement. Ranghar became suspicious. There was a deep dry drain. A lot of husk was spread here and there around it as the harvests had been cut. Ranghar drove away the mule towards it and hid himself under the hush.

Some peasants were tilling their fields nearby. Ranga went to them and said. "Will you please sell this hush? I need it." The tillers said, "It is useless for us. You take it away," but Ranga paid them five rupees as a token money.

Ranga set the hush on fire and sat in a corner. He was sure that Ranghar would meet his death and he would handle the money later on.

The husk was not fully denied up. There was smoke and smoke all around. Ranghar was sure that Ranga was following him. The fire could be the work of Ranga's fertile mind. Ranghar sped away with the mule under the darkness of thick smoke. Later on Ranga thrashed the ash but there was no trace of Ranghar's burnt up boxes and silver coins. Ranga was not disappointed. He followed Ranghar's foot-steps.

Ranga side tracked Ranghar and went to a nearby village, he knew Ranghar's weakness. He bought a beautiful pair of shoes. He dropped a single shoe on Ranghar's path. When Ranghar came he was sorry to see only one shoe. He did not care and proceeded onward. He had hardly gone half a mile he noticed the second shoe. He was tempted. Ranga's bait worked. He went back to pickup the shoe tying the mule with a bush. Now it was Ranga's turn. He came out of the bushes and fled away with the mule. When Ranghar returned he felt a humiliating rebuff at Ranga's hand.

Ranga reached his home with full load of silver coins. He unloaded the mule and set it free for jungle. He related the whole episode to his wife and said, "If Ranghar comes, strike your head on his chest. Ask about my where abouts. Accuse him for my murder. Weep bitterly so that neighbours may gather and Ranghar may get frightened. He further said, "I shall hide in that Jhera or dried up well. You supply me food there by hanging a rope. Be bold."

Ranga left for the nearby dried up well. When Ranghar came to Ranga house his wife acted as advised by her husband. She struck her head against Ranghar and asked about her husband's well being and whereabout. Ranga's wife asked Rangher to trace him out as soon as possible.

Ranghar hid himself in the village and followed the movements of Ranga's wife. He noted that she goes to a nearby dried up well and drops food through a rope in it. He was amused and thought a plan to loot Ranga.

Next day he arranged food for Ranga and reached the well before his wife could reach. He dropped the food through rope. Ranga said, "Why this food is so dry and without vegetables?" Ranghar spoke like Ranga's wife and said, "I have no money." Ranga said, "A lot of money is hidden under the Chakki or millstone. What about the money which I brought on the laden mule. "Mimicking his wife's voice Ranghar said." I shall bring best food tomorrow."

Then Ranga's wife came as usual and dropped food through the rope. Ranga was surprised. He said, "Why food for the second time? His wife said, "What are you saying? I am here for the first time."

Ranga said, "He must be Ranghar. Be careful. Take me out. Let us rush back to home. He must have looted our money by now."

When they returned home they found everything topsy-turvy. Ranghar looted his hidden money as well as the money brought on the mule. He rushed to his home along with the laden mule.

Ranghar's wife was overjoyed to see countless money.

Ranghar warned his wife and said, "Ranga will come. Tell him that my husband returned from your house. Your have poisoned him. He is dead. I will file a suit against you."

Ranghar smoked his hookah. He covered himself with a white chaddar as if he was wrapped in a coffin, he had a sound sleep.

On the other hand Ranga followed Ranghar. He could trace the hoof steps of the mule as it was heavily loaden. When he reached Ranghar's house his wife began to weep bitterly. She accused Ranga for her husband's death. Ranga took it cool.

The villagers arranged Ranghar's last ceremony. When they were ready to take him to the funeral place Ranga said, "He was my best friend. I want to see his face. Let me pray for his soul. I shall stand along with his bier." All left them alone.

Ranga said, "O my friend Ranghar, let us divide the money in two halves equally. Too much greed is harmful otherwise you will turn to ashes."

Ranghar showed no reaction as if he was completely dead. His bier was borne by Ranga also. As a rite when Ranghar's bier was put to rest midway Ranga uncovered his face and requested for a fair division of the money.

❄ ❄ ❄

Glossary

Adhai Chhail	:	Two and a half times handsome
Amavasya	:	15th day of dark fortnight
Badashah	:	King
Bali ka Bakra	:	A goat for the sacrifice
Bhatai	:	Brother of the woman who gives gifts at the Wedding Ceremony
Bhathiyarin	:	A female inn-keeper
Chakki	:	Grinding device of stones
Charaka and Lukman	:	Vaid/Hakim of old times
Chaupal	:	A meeting place in the village
Chhathi	:	Sixth day of birth ceremony
Chhuchhak	:	Gifts from married girl's parents on the birth of the child
Chopaaies	:	Couplets
Daal	:	Pulse/Lentil
Dedh Chhail	:	One and a half times dandy
Ganga Snan	:	Holy bath in river Ganga
Ghunghurus	:	Small bells fixed on a cloth or leather belt
Grihipravesh	:	Entrance Ceremony in the new house
Hakeem	:	Unani Doctor
Halwaai	:	A sweets-maker
Henna	:	Mehndi
Hookah	:	Smoking tobacco device through water

Jachcha	:	A woman who delivered a child recently
Jajmaan	:	One who pays for services
Kaliyuga	:	Age of bad-period of time, the last *yuga*
Karuwa Tamaku	:	Bitter Tobacco
Laddoos	:	Popular Indian sweet
Lokas	:	Abodes of souls
Mogri	:	Wooden hammer used for spinning
Pitraas	:	Deceased fore-fathers
Pindas	:	A ceremony for the deceased person
Purohit	:	Priest (Pandit)
Sagaai	:	Betroth ceremony
Sayana	:	Soothsayer
Seawa Rupyaa	:	One rupee and 25 paise
Shraddh	:	Offering food, clothes to departed soul every year
Sitaphal	:	Pumpkin
Teli	:	Who extracts oil
Tulsi	:	A shrub, sacred basil plant
Vaidyaji	:	Ayurvedic Doctor
Wazir	:	Minister